H45 213 033

D1485525

0 MAY 2000

19 ; 2000

1 7 APR 2001

-8 NOV 2001

- 2 JAN 2003

1 6 JAN 2003
3 0 JAN 2003

2 9 MAY 2003
2 6 JUN 2003

2 0 DEC 2005

2 4 JAN 2006
- 4 MAY 2006
1 0 AUG 2006

- 3 OCT 2006

10 JAN 2007

- 5 APR 2007
2 6 APR 2007

L32a   1 9 MAY 2001

Please renew/return this item by the last date shown.

So that your telephone call is charged at local rate,
please call the numbers as set out below:

	From Area codes 01923 or 0208:	From the rest of Herts:
Renewals:	01923 471373	01438 737373
Enquiries:	01923 471333	01438 737333
Minicom:	01923 471599	01438 737599

L32b

2 2 APR 1999

TUPPENCE FOR THE RAINBOW

TUPPENCE
FOR THE RAINBOW

The Story of a Bradford Lad

by

Leslie Sands

Bradford Libraries and Information Service

First Published in 1990
Bradford Libraries and Information Service

A Ryburn Book Production
Composed in Monotype Plantin
by Ryburn Typesetting Ltd,
Luddendenfoot, Halifax
Printed by Dotesios Printers Ltd,
Trowbridge, Wiltshire

British Library Cataloguing in Publication Data
Sands, Leslie
    Tuppence for the Rainbow: the story of a Bradford lad.
    1. (Metropolitan County) West Yorkshire.
    Bradford. Social life, history. Biographies.
    I. Title II. Bradford Libraries and Information Service
    942.817092

    ISBN: 0-907734-22-7

Contents

Illustrations

Acknowledgements

Many people have helped me to get the story of my early years published. I would like to give my thanks to Bradford Libraries and Information Service for undertaking the task, and to its Reference Librarian, Bob Duckett, for the picture research and the final preparation of the text. My thanks also to Sally Wolfe of the library for her help with production and publicity matters. Peter Holdsworth of the Bradford *Telegraph & Argus* dug out some interesting old photographs and I gratefully acknowledge his help and the paper's kindness in allowing me to use them. Many thanks to Richard Clark and his staff at Ryburn Book Production for the excellent end-product of all our endeavours.

Leslie Sands

October 1990

For Our Alb

Chapter One

──────────── ❖ ────────────

Focus

Usually Dad and I would sit there for about an hour, while the old lady slowly and very grudgingly made up her mind. Sometimes it was more than that; sometimes, but very rarely, less. Grandma Sands knew above all things how to keep you waiting.

'How much is it this time?' she'd ask, though she knew the answer perfectly well. 'How much did you say?'

'Half a dollar, Ma. Just till I draw me dole.'

There would be a lull, as her face went sour. It was my grandma who first taught me the value of the dramatic pause, though I have never been able to use it as well or hold it for as long as she did. Finally: 'I don't know, Albert,' and she would shake her great head in open condemnation of her eldest son, 'I – just – don't – know.' Then would come a deep sigh. When Grandma Sands sighed, you quivered. When she sighed deeply, the earth shook. It had good reason to, for although she was of only average height she weighed more than fourteen stone. The massive jowls would wobble with the dying hiss of the sigh; the fleshy lips would purse as if she were in secret pain, and be slowly moistened by the sinuous pink tongue; then she would relapse into a silence of martyred gloom. But her hands kept busy. I never knew her when she wasn't active on some household task, although when we were there she would make sure this was some sitting-down job which enabled her to use her time effectively without losing one jot of her monumental authority.

'Two bob, then?' My dad's grey eyes would look frank and appealing; he was as good an actor as she was, if not better. But I knew he was acting for my benefit as well, for under the superficial patience and good humour there always lurked a sense of strain, as he wondered anxiously if it would work this time or if – this time – his mother would say no. And our need was pressing. 'Go on, Ma, you can easy manage a couple o' bob.'

'I don't know what you do with your money.'

'There isn't any. That's why we're here, me and our Les.' This was a deliberate ploy, on his part. She had a soft spot for me, and that was why he almost invariably took me with him on these cadging trips. It was also why, every single time, he perched me on the black horsehair sofa that was in her direct line of view; the prickles on it were sharp, and dug into the backs of your bare knees like miniature daggers.

'You never come to see me for nowt else.' This would be delivered with an assumed bitterness and, to reassure me, Dad might throw me a wink on what he imagined was his safe side. 'And you needn't wink at that lad when you think I'm not looking!' The old battle-axe missed nothing.

In the late twenties and early thirties, when these calls at the little shop in Barkerend Road took place with depressing regularity, there was nothing strange to my young mind about the lengthy and humiliating procedure they entailed. Everybody in the North was hard up then, and some were starving. My birthplace, Bradford in Yorkshire, lay at the centre of a rut of despair that stretched from the coalfields of Wales up to the great shipyards of Tyneside and the Clyde. In those days you went where you could to get the brass: if you couldn't work for it, you had to borrow; if the borrowing wasn't easy, you had to beg; and if the begging failed, you stole. Not that these long-drawn-out visits ever struck me as any form of begging. There is something impersonal and withdrawn about your true beggar, whereas this was a very personal and intimate affair indeed. That hunched and hulking figure in the long black dress, with the mop of untidy silvery hair above the stern and almost masculine features, was my own grandmother.

A typical corner shop: this one was in Britannia Street c.1930.
Photo: Bradford Libraries and Information Service

My flesh and blood. She'd brought my dad up in these rooms behind the shop, the eldest boy in a family of eight children, all of whom she bullied and adored. She had found us our first independent home, not far away from her own. At that juncture she organised and dominated all her vast brood like some great and godlike eminence. Grandma Sands knew best, about everything. But she saw to it that she was never the loser in her apparent acts of kindness to the spreading clan. If you borrowed money from her, and Albert Edward wasn't the only one by a long chalk, her rate of interest – levied on family and strangers alike – was one penny per shilling per week. And she always collected it.

'When do you think you'll pay it back?'

'Soon as I can.'

'You live in a dream world, lad.' This was truer than she suspected: he was a dreamer by nature, and would remain a lad all his life.

Their slight verbal exchanges were spare, spaced-out and invariably acidic. I kept my ten-year-old trap shut and left it to my father, watching him carefully over the months in which he gradually became an expert at the job of extracting money from her.

He was of average height and had a squarish face, sallow in complexion and deeply lined beyond his years, a legacy from the trenches in France. His figure was stocky and he had the chest and shoulders of a young bull. He was undoubtedly good-looking and yet his chief attraction lay in his keen sense of humour and his irrepressible personality. He dressed as smartly as his limited resources would allow, and was clean-shaven all the days I knew him. His grin was irresistible.

At length she was bound to ask: 'How's our Alice?'

'Same as ever. Towing her heart out at home.'

'Women have to tow their hearts out. Born to it.'

'Aye.' You never argued with that, not in the North.

'She hasn't been round here since I don't know when.'

'She'll come when she's ready,' Dad would assure her. 'She sends her love.'

'That won't pay many bills.'

When she lay on her death-bed in years to come, it would be Alice she asked for to keep her company, to light her a last cigarette and to make sure she had a decent laying-out.

Alice, my mother, would be round the corner in Grant Street, hoping that her husband's quest might meet with some success. She was a tiny lady, who barely cleared five feet, with a darkish complexion, luxuriant chestnut-coloured hair and large and luminous brown eyes that were as honest as the day is long. Throughout her life those eyes reflected faithfully her every thought and feeling, for she was quite incapable of any form of deceit. Mum shared my dad's sense of humour, though her wit was not as quick as his. She also shared his every fear and apprehension. She was as nervous about our economic state as he was, but had the uncompromising honesty to show it openly. The dole was going to be reduced, it said in the papers, and Grandma Sands wouldn't put up with this borrowing lark for ever. But whether Albert brought anything back with him or not, she'd have to manage somehow. She always had, and always would. So she would laugh away her anxieties, and say if you were a mill-lass at heart, a *real* mill-lass, you never let Life get you down. And she always got the better of it, even in the stricken West Riding of the years round 1931.

'She'll be waiting, Ma.'

'I won't be rushed.'

'We've got nowt for us tea. We need coal an' all, if you could spare another bob.' Household coal was one pound a ton, and you could get a hundredweight sack of chunky cobs for a shilling. That could keep you going for a fortnight, if you were careful to eke it out with damp slack and briquettes made from coal-dust, cinders and tightly screwed-up sheets of newspaper.

Dad would muster a hopeful smile, but his stubby fingers would be plucking restlessly now at the creases in his blue serge trousers that were always shiny at the knees. She wasn't going to soften this time. This time, she'd had enough. What was left? He had three hungry mouths to feed, but what the hell could you do without a job? Nothing. Except – give her another ten minutes. And go on, cross your fingers. She might be made of granite, but she liked to see a smiling face: so grin your heart out, might as well. Talk about laugh clown, bloody laugh!

The room would seem to grow bigger and more hostile as time passed on. I would look round, growing restive as the minutes dragged slowly by. The old coats behind the door to the back yard gave off their usual reek of damp and mildew. The wall-paper was stained and greasy, and the heavy Edwardian pictures weighed you down with an excess of gloom. Through the open arch, leading to the shop in front and Grandad's little bench out there, seeped the tang of new leather and the faintly off-putting odour of sweaty boots and shoes, in for soling and heeling. On the huge, black chiffonier the little china ornaments that were part of Grandma's extensive collection of seaside souvenirs glinted pathetically at you, reflecting the small flames dancing in the grate of the kitchen range. The giant cast-iron kettle on the hob hummed and sizzled as it always did when I was there, but we were rarely offered a cup of tea on these strictly business visits.

This room would see me again at various stages of my early life: as a toiling schoolboy, a know-all undergraduate, a would-be actor, a disgruntled serviceman and, eventually, a dry-eyed mourner. I was never to forget it.

'How's young Albert doing at secondary school?'

'All right, far as we know. He doesn't say much.'

Young Albert was my elder brother and personal idol.

'A lot o' lads are out at work at his age, bringing summat in.'

'Good luck to 'em. I was a worker long before that, wasn't I? Half-timing, at twelve years old.' Dad's eyes could go flinty too when he wanted them to. 'Missed me chance, I did. My lads aren't going to miss theirs.'

'All talk.'

'Go on, Ma. Eighteenpence? Be a sport.'

'Fine example you set 'em. Out o' work, and round here every verse-end, tapping me for money – '

'I'm not the only one who hasn't got a job.'

In the early nineteen-thirties there were nearly three million unemployed in Britain. In our area, one man in four was out of a job; in Wales, more than one in three. Hearts were festering with bitterness down on the Rhondda and up in Jarrow.

Dad would be on the point of giving up and she would know it, but she had to ram home her advantage to the full. This never failed to give her a strange satisfaction.

'I'll have to be off. She'll be worried to death.' He might even get up on his feet to stress the point.

'Alice knows where you've got to, don't you fret. Still ... none of it's her fault, I suppose ...' He had struck a responsive chord at last. Now the secret society of womanhood would operate on his behalf. 'Poor lass!' The busy hands would come to rest for a telling moment, indicating the ordeal was almost over. 'Fool to meself, that's what I am.' Thick fingers would grope unhurriedly in a bulging handbag, and a little pile of coins would be measured out carefully on the scrubbed table-top. 'There y'are then – two bob. And I want that back at t'week-end, don't forget!'

'Right! Come on, Les.'

His cloth cap would be pulled on again immediately, at its usual jaunty angle; and the thought of Wild Woodbines soon to come would make his movements light and agile. He would never show the relief he felt, but always remembered to throw her a farewell grin.

'Thanks, Ma.'

'I should think so, an' all!' was all he'd get from her.

We never used to stay long, once the cash was out of her bag and into his pocket. Out through the little shop we'd go: 'Ta-ra, Dad.' 'Ta-ra, Grandad!' The wizened figure would be clamped on its stool in the cobbler's cubby-hole, hammering leather on footwear. Grandad Sands's clenched mouth was always a bright semicircle of brass tacks, all waiting to be plucked out and banged in one by one, so that he could only mumble and grimace at us in reply. The hanging bell would clang as we opened the shop-door, and tinkle faintly as we closed it again behind us.

'Two bob, Dad. Not bad, eh?'

'No. We caught her in a good mood for once. But think on, that two bob was only eighteenpence if your mother asks. Here's a penny.'

'Ta!' The coin would be eagerly received and promptly tucked away in the pocket of my grey flannel shorts. It would buy me one of my favourite comics, *Larks* perhaps, *Comic Cuts*, or *The Jester*. If I could build it up to tuppence, that would get me *The Rainbow*, more expensive than its fellows because it was larger and some of its pages were printed in full colour.

The eighteenpence would often have to last us for a couple of days, until the next time Dad went down to what we called 'The Labour'; but my mother could make a few coppers go further than anyone I have ever known. What he had kept back for himself would buy his beer over the same period. Tetley's

Bitter cost twopence a half-pint in those days; and in it Dad had found his own Rainbow, his personal escape into a brighter world.

The tickling and smarting would still be there at the backs of my legs, where the old horsehair sofa had left its mark. Dad always kept a stern eye on how we behaved, out in the street. 'Stop scratching yourself! Folk'll think you're loppy.'

Then we would break into a trot together, jog past the Red House on the corner (ignored for the moment as it wasn't yet opening-time) and travel down Garnett Street, often hand in hand, to our home in Grant Street. His Alice would be there, waiting for him. She always was. She always would be. And she smiled a lot more often than his mother – especially when he had eighteenpence to hold out to her.

These interviews with Grandma Sands stand out in my memory as an abiding image of the Hungry Thirties. They were a contributory factor to the insecurity that has haunted me all my life, and will be with me until I die.

Chapter Two

❖

Breeding-ground

I first saw the light of day in that little house in Grant Street, one mile from the heart of the city, less than three years after the end of the Great War. My mother often told the tale with gusto:

> I remember it was early on this Thursday morning, and I went across the yard to t'lavatory to empty slops. I was just coming back with the big bucket when this damned great rat came under the midden door and scuttled off down the passage. I screamed out loud – couldn't help it! I'd seen rats before and plenty of 'em, but never one as big as that. He was a roster. It was then I got the pains. They were bad. We had to send for Albert, get him out of work – he went straight round for t'midwife.

Later the same Thursday I was born, weighing over twelve pounds, without eyelashes or eyebrows and, according to my mother, with no evidence of finger-nails either. I turned out to be a roster, too. When people ask me nowadays what my stars are, I tell them I was born under the Sign of the Rat – and leave it at that.

My father was a Yorkshireman, born and bred. But his father, Albert Sands, had come up from Worcestershire during the agricultural depression of the late nineteenth century, to seek a living as a maker and mender of boots and shoes among the thriving wool-mills of the industrial North.

The cobbler met his match in the formidable Annie Chanter, my Grandma Sands. She was a lady of tremendous strength of character, who always took a conscious pride in her own family background. Her mother had once run a private school, and her father had been a respected guard on the early railways.

	Sugden, Charles, engineer	BURNSALL MOUNT.
186	Walter, F., pork butcher	316 Milner, A., umbrella mfr.
188	Taylor, B. R., confectioner	*Curzon road*
190	Watson, L., confectioner	BILSON MOUNT.
192	Atkinson, Leah, caterer	320 Pickles, F., mixed bus.
194	Sands, Albert, boot repairer	*Fitzroy road*
196	Wheelhouse, M. J., gnrl. dlr.	324 Pitchers, R. T., joiner and
198	Wheelhouse, M. J., peas, pies, etc.	undertaker
200	Seavers, E., *Red House Inn*	330 Blackburn, W. H., shipping merchant
	Garnett street	334a Bottomley, G. H., butcher
208,	210 Clark, A. Wm., mixed business	*Pillar Box*

My grandfather Albert Sands listed at 194 Barkerend Road in *The Post Office Bradford Directory* of 1928.

Courtesy of Bradford Libraries and Information Service

'I wasn't always a shoemaker's wife, you know,' she would remind you. 'Oh, no. By, I could tell you some tales ... when I was a lass, in that great big house. Eh, dear – if these lips could only speak!'

But speak they did, quite often; and when they spoke, people listened. One of her cherished reminiscences was that of a girlhood sweetheart, ill-educated, who had risen by sheer determination to be a youthful Mayor of Bradford. At his inaugural banquet, being unsure of protocol and which knives and forks he should properly use, he had specially requested that his old flame Annie should sit by his side to keep a weather eye on him. This she did gladly, for she always loved any form of ceremony. At the end of the meal they compared notes.

'How d'it go then, lad? Everything all right?'

'Champion, Annie. One thing though – I thought them prunes was a bit sour.'

'Did you now?' Annie Chanter had smiled a secret smile.

'Aye. Too sour, them prunes. Too hard, an' all.'

'I'm not surprised,' she told him. 'You see, them prunes was pickled walnuts.'

Be that as it may, Albert Sands and his fashionably buxom wife set up house together at 194 Barkerend Road, Bradford and in due course raised their brood of eight. Their first child was a daughter, Ethel. Then came their first son. He was christened Albert Edward, and was one day to become my father. Albert Edward surprised the neighbourhood by showing marked ability when he was at school. But with a growing family to tend, and only one struggling cobbler's meagre earnings to provide for them, his mother made him start work at the age of twelve. So he became a 'half-timer', working half the day in the mill and enjoying the other half in studies and football at Barkerend School. At fourteen he left school for good, and the bang and clatter of the mill claimed all his time.

My mother, Alice Riley, was the second daughter of Tom Riley and his bride, Sarah Ann Widdop, Bradfordians and millhands both. Alice too was put out to work – full-time, in her case – at twelve years old, for this was well in advance of the days of compassionate laws governing child labour. She worked in the mill as a bobbin-minder, from dawn till dusk, for a pittance. As long as she lived, she would recall endless journeys on foot to the great, clattering buildings in early morning light, traversing the narrow streets and lanes with her hand clasped tightly in that of her elder sister, Nelly. Both children were so dog-tired that each took it in turn to keep her eyes open and guide the other up and down steps and round corners, while the second unfortunate's eyes were still tight shut, as she stumbled along in a half-coma.

My father and mother met in the mill, where they courted each other from the age of fourteen onwards.

On 4 August 1914 war came, and within a month my father had responded to the call of duty, spurred on by the brass bands, the bristling recruiting sergeants and the patriotic fervour of the times. He enlisted in September 1914 as an infantryman in the sixteenth battalion of the West Yorkshire regiment, the renowned 'Bradford Pals'.

The shop at 194 Barkerend Road as it is today.

Photo © Ian Beesley

Before he went off on active service, Albert Edward married Alice at Holy Trinity Church in Leeds Road, Bradford. Their first son – yet another Albert – would be born the following year. At the time of their marriage the young husband was nineteen and his radiant bride some six months older. On a shilling a day, he was then engaged in initial training on

Salisbury Plain, but was soon destined as a foot-slogger for the arid wastes of Mesopotamia and, within months, for the frightfulness of the Western Front. He would eventually rise to the rank of quartermaster-sergeant and be mentioned in despatches for conspicuous bravery in the field. Meanwhile, he would be near the River Somme in the plain of Picardy, on the morning of 3 July, 1916.

On that date, the British red-tabs sent their biggest force ever into action, consisting of twenty six full divisions. Every man who went over the top at the Battle of the Somme was a volunteer, and every ranker was heavily laden with nearly seventy pounds of cumbersome equipment. Before the day was out, the British had suffered 60,000 casualties and the two battalions of the Bradford Pals had been almost totally wiped out. My father was one of the few survivors.

He was finally demobilised in 1919, and went to live with his wife and son at the home of her parents in Seaton Street, up Bradford Moor. Albert junior, by then nearly four years old, was a thin, sensitive and pallid child, susceptible to illness due to the hardships of wartime birth and feeding. He can recall to this day lying in his cot at Seaton Street during the war years, before he could properly talk:

> My Grandma Riley had this little bird in a cage, Les.
> Little yellow bird. Later on I knew it for a canary. The
> sun was shining and I just laid there, watching it. It
> was singing. Then the singing stopped. It sort of shook
> itself, and fell – fell sideways, off its perch. Then
> everything was still and quiet, but the sun still shone.
> They told me it was dead, but I didn't know what that
> meant; so they said it had gone to Jesus. Funny, I've
> only got to close my eyes and I can hear it singing still.

That's my brother – in his mid-seventies now – reliving his earliest memory.

In 1920, Albert Edward's mother found the little family the first home of their own, in a cul-de-sac round the corner called Grant Street. By this time her son was a corporation labourer, and this appears as his occupation on the birth certificate of his second son, Tom Leslie, born there on 19 May 1921.

The house, in the little street's only back yard, was Number 11. Downstairs, it had one main room and a scullery, and both of these had floors that were made of stone. Stone steps led up to the two bedrooms above. And that was my breeding-ground. It had no bathroom, no inside lavatory and certainly very little intrinsic warmth or comfort; but within those walls, I had the warmest and finest upbringing any lad could have.

The single downstairs window looked out on the yard. Slap opposite the front door was the midden into which all the household refuse was emptied, to be dug out once a week by men who wore tightly-knotted string below their knees to make stray rodents keep their distance. Next to the midden was the outside water-closet which we shared with some neighbours from the house 'in front' – that is, in Grant Street proper. And next to the lavatory, in the very corner of our yard, was a soaring mill-chimney built of red bricks, that served the exploited effort in the sweatshops beyond. For we were in the heartland of the back-to-backs, the tiny stone dwellings built by the rich mill-owners of the Industrial Revolution to house their teeming and ill-paid minions within sight and earshot of their place of labour.

They say I didn't learn to talk until I was over two.

'There's summat wrong wi' that lad,' my dad would declare, 'He never says a word. Not a blind word!'

'He'll make up for it when he's older,' my mum would reassure him. 'For now, he's taking it all in.'

'Likes his grub. He'll probably end up as a cook in a home for the deaf and dumb.'

The first room I remember is the living-room where I was born. The fire in the grate is one of my earliest recollections. It formed the central feature of our black-leaded range: to the left of it was a small, square oven with a large round knob; on its right was our only source of hot water, a cast-iron boiler whose contents, for some forgotten reason, were always a frothy grey. On the lid of the boiler stood a 'layding-can', a sturdy utensil with a wide handle and a broad and generous spout. Water was taken by means of this across the room and into the tiny and frigid scullery, where the family performed its limited ablutions. To the left of the fireplace, the alcove formed by the chimney-breast had been converted into two cupboards, the 'top' and the 'low'. The top cupboard held all the household crockery and supplies; the low cupboard was given over to a higgledy-piggledy collection of old clothes, worn out but possibly still usable boots and shoes, and the children's simple and mostly home-made toys. In the alcove on the right of the fire was an oval-topped, walnut stand that did duty as a sideboard. Over this, proudly framed and displayed, were Dad's medals and the certificate from the War Office that quoted his mention in despatches. In one corner was the chamber-door, opening on to the stone steps that led up to the bedrooms. Upstairs, things were rather spartan. Dad and Mother had the larger room, which boasted a double bed with a brass bedstead, a big and clammy cupboard for clothes, a tin trunk for family documents and (always, in my early youth) a large tin bucket for the purpose of nocturnal relief.

'Alice – pretty buttercup!' my dad would yell out from aloft; this always meant 'Bring the bucket up.'

Once I was out of long clothes and dummy-teats, Albert and I slept in the smaller room. Half of this extended over the open passage below, and as a result the place was always cold. Its walls were covered in distemper of a shade my brother used to call 'institution green'. Our clothes hung on hooks behind the bedroom door and were covered in sheets of brown paper. Our bedside table was an orange-box stood on its end and covered in flowered wallpaper. This held our candlestick, as the gas-fitting in there was unreliable, and Albert's spectacles, magazines and books.

I cannot remember when my father switched from corporation labouring to cloth-shrinking at a firm called Holt's (at the blind end of our little street), but I do recall we knew great happiness throughout those early years. There were many sunlit days when I was in the house alone with my mother, while Dad was out at work and Albert was up at Barkerend Elementary School, studying hard so that he might one day taste the joys of secondary education.

I sat one day playing at Crusaders, using the raised end of the green velvet sofa as my horse and wearing an old trilby hat of my father's, which had been cut down and trimmed to form a medieval helmet. My mother clanked and banged busily in the scullery, singing a popular song of the day called *Moonlight and Roses*. The memory is clear of being supremely happy in the innocence of early childhood. Sometimes nowadays I hear the tune played on nostalgia programmes; and I am back immediately, bouncing on that sofa-end and chasing those hated Turks again.

'Mind them springs, Les – sofas don't come two a penny!'

As the early cinema grew in popularity, the game of Cowboys and Indians came into fashion. Every lad had his imaginary horse, and some of the older ones wore cowboy 'sets' and swung and juggled their cap-pistols with tremendous dexterity. I was upstairs one day in my parent's bedroom being Tom Mix, and on this occasion using one of the top rails on their bedstead as my bounding steed. Enthusiasm got the better of me and I strained forward hard, whipping my horse Tony with my hand and whooping out loud, not knowing I was in some personal danger. Magnificent as it seemed to Albert and me compared with our old iron bedstead, the brass one was of advanced years and had started to disintegrate. The two halves of one of its knobs were coming apart, opening up dangerous cutting edges. It was over one of these that I stretched my crotch at the climax of my make-believe round-up. Suddenly I felt a sharp pain between my legs and, when I looked, saw dark red oozing through the woolly pants I was wearing.

My mother was down below, sharing a cup of tea with my godmother Auntie Ethel. Both flew upstairs at once in answer to my screeches of pain and fright, and rapidly ministered to my needs. What was always referred to in my childhood as my 'dickie' had been badly slashed, and was bleeding copiously. Ointment was plastered all over the damaged member by my mother, and a primitive bandage was hastily applied by my concerned aunt. 'He's always in the wars, our Les,' she commented, as she tied the bandage and made me wince. I was weeping salt tears that were partly a result of the hurt, but mainly due to my acute embarrassment. 'He'll never make a soldier!' The tears returned whenever the incident cropped up within the growing Sands family, who seemed to take a delight in discussing it at social gatherings for a long time after. My godfather Uncle Percy, who fancied himself as a wag, always waited carefully for the right moment and then would announce (as if he had just thought of it): 'Good job he didn't rip it right off, eh? Poor look-out for the honeymoon!' I had no idea what he meant but it usually made everybody laugh, and thus increased my sense of shame.

Since the day the accident happened, I have always been shy of displaying myself in public. This has mystified several doctors in my lifetime, upset one or two amorous ladies, making them doubt their charms, and was a distinct drawback during my years in the Services, when 'flashing it round' on request or demand (or even for purposes of simple comparison) was something of a social obligation.

I was given as consolation a little toy gramophone, housed in a small, cream-painted cabinet. The single record that came with it was of a melody called *Narcissus*. Just as *Moonlight and Roses* always fills me with warm content, so *Narcissus* never fails to bring a sharp stab of fancied agony where one would least desire it.

I had few playmates when very young, and my greatest friend was my brother Albert. He was six years older than I, and in his early youth somewhat frail and prone to frequent ailment. He had impaired eyesight, and from his very early days had to wear spectacles. When he was fit and well though, we would have great games together. Soldiers was my favourite, when we would don various representations of tin hats, and shoot at each other with cap-guns across the room from fancied shell-holes. Old 'pumps' (plimsolls) and rubber balls would magically transform themselves into missiles and hand-grenades. We usually played this game when Dad was out at the pub though, because he always disapproved of it when he was there.

'We've had enough of bloody war,' he would tell us blackly. 'Play summat else.'

So when he was in the room we would fall back on cigarette-cards, fingering our hordes of the little pasteboard oblongs greedily and then 'scaging' them through the air to lie in a competitive heap near the low cupboard door. 'Taws' (otherwise marbles) were another great diversion, as was the game of tiddlywinks, until all the coloured counters got lost, stolen or unaccountably strayed. Outside in the yard we played cricket, though I was never any good at this and Albert always won. When this palled, we would chalk a board up on the midden-door and throw darts at it, darts Dad had 'won' from the pub.

Albert was taking an interest in comics and boys' magazines now; I could not read the writing but I loved looking at the pictures, and was always on at him to tell me the stories that accompanied them.

'Give us a chance, Les,' he used to protest, 'Just give us time to *read* 'em!'

In Garnett Street, across the road from the end of our cul-de-sac, was the large house and business premises of Mr Pickles, a manufacturer of mineral waters or 'pop', as we knew it then. Mr Pickles had a charming and attractive wife and two bouncing, fair-haired daughters. Regrettably, Mrs Pickles could have no more children, much as she may have wanted them. And her husband had always longed for a boy of his own, someone he could inspire and train and who, when the right moment came, would take over the firm and carry the name of Pickles down to posterity. If he happened on the right sort of lad, he could afford to be generous in the matter of adoption terms: the ready-made son would have a comfortable and secure life, a happy home, an assured future and all the pop he could drink. This last would not have cost old Pickles much, for it was his oft-repeated boast that he could turn the whole of Bradford Moor Park Lake into lemonade 'for not much more than a quid'.

When I was three years old they caught sight of me playing out in Grant Street, and Mr Pickles thought that he had found just the lad he wanted for his son and heir. Advances were made, and my mother and dad considered the proposition in half-seriousness.

'Our Les 'ud grow up well off; he'd never go without,' I heard my father say. 'Besides, Pickles says he'll make it worth us while.'

'They're not having my lad.'

'Just think. It might help send our Alb on to Hanson Secondary. He's keen on that, and so am I.'

'What about our Les?' my mother demanded, 'Where's he going to end up?'

'Aw, Pickles would put him in a private school – Woodhouse Grove, somewhere posh like that. He'd never *want*, Alice.'

'I said no and I mean it.' Mum stuck her chin out.

'It might help us to move.' As his mother would, my dad was considering all aspects before finally making up his mind. 'It's dear here, for what it is.' His rent was three shillings and elevenpence a week; but then, his weekly wages were less than two pounds sterling. 'Make a big difference, I can tell you.'

'They're not having my lad, not at any price. And you ought to be ashamed of yourself – for considering it.'

Dad thought about this for a moment, and then slapped her on the bottom. 'I'm only pulling your leg.'

I had been listening, and I was tremendously relieved. They had explained to me what 'adoption' meant before they started talking, and I had been shaking in my shoes.

Anyway, that was that. Mr Pickles's dreams of a dynasty remained unfulfilled. He died a rich man and, as far as I know, Pick-Up Minerals died with him.

One of his biggest competitors in that part of the West Riding was a firm called Thompson and Pearson, who had a fleet of horses and carts to ply their trade round the scores of pubs and working-men's clubs in the area. Their slogan, painted in scarlet edged with silver wherever space could be found, was 'Drink T. and P. Mineral Waters'. This always looked mightily impressive until the day Dad gave it his own individual interpretation.

'Don't you see what it means, none of you? Say it out loud – go on – "DRINK TEA AND PEE MINERAL WATERS." They ought to have more sense!'

There came a time when the latest arrival in the Sands family decided to strike out on his own. Let my brother set the scene for me.

Well, if memory serves me right Les, that was the summer of 1924. I remember that particular time very well. And it was a beautiful day: school holidays, and we were having a bit of a heat-wave. I think me and the lads were sitting on the causeway, up near Holt's offices. And you came out of the passage. You must have been looking for me, but you didn't see me. I remember the suit you were wearing: it was a little cotton suit, little blouse and trousers in pink and white squares. White socks, with red or pink tops, and some little red shoes. And you had your golden curly hair. Haven't got that any more, have you, lad? Anyway, you came out of that passage and you never saw me. So you set off down Grant Street, up Garnett Street and subsequently along Barkerend Road. You must have been walking down the main road by yourself and there was this copper – a bobby on horseback. He picked you up and you got a ride on his horse.

I don't know when or why I left the house. It must have been in the morning and my mother would be out shopping, knowing Albert wasn't very far away. Perhaps I was hoping to find her; perhaps I went out searching for my brother as he says, for I always dogged his footsteps then; or perhaps I was just feeling a bit adventurous. I do have a half-memory of the long and busy road, with reflections of myself in the grimy

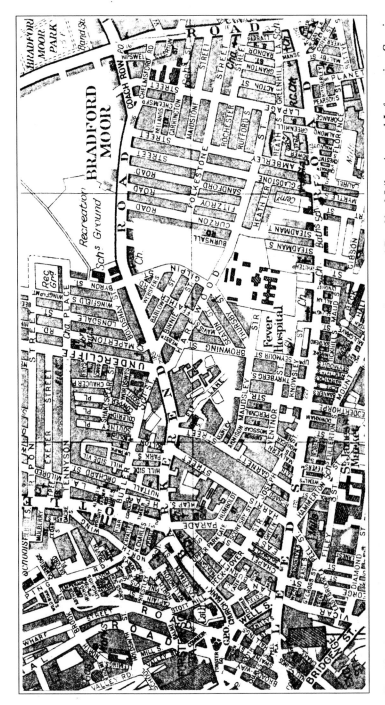

Bradford city centre and Barkerend Road 1938.

Courtesy of Bradford Libraries and Information Service

shop windows as I marched along; and I don't remember feeling the least bit frightened or out of my depth. Nobody seemed to take any notice for a while of a little lad toddling into the unknown through the summer sunshine. I have a clearer recollection of being scooped up suddenly from the ground, and strong arms – I think they were feminine – passing me up to the policeman on an enormous brown horse with a long, black mane. After that, my memory goes blank.

All hell broke loose when Mother got back and found me missing. Neighbours were called in to help and a search was mounted throughout the local streets and snickets. It met with no success. Nobody remembered seeing a three-year-old out on his solitary travels that bright morning.

Grandma Sands was duly informed, as she had to be on all occasions, and gave it as her considered opinion that I had been kidnapped. God knows what kind of ransom the kidnappers were hoping to get out of us! 'Go to Holt's. Fetch Albert out o' work and get down to that Town Hall, fast as you can.'

This must have struck dread into my poor mother's heart. The Town Hall was a tall, forbidding structure, soot-encrusted, that bestrode Town Hall Square and was a place of civic dignitaries, magistrates' courts, rate-offices and police involvement. You went there only if you were in trouble for non-payment of dues and demands and had been 'summonsed'; or perhaps if you were taken there by force in the Black Maria, and clapped into a cell when you hadn't been behaving yourself properly. The looming Town Hall was a necessary but unloved menace.

However, when Dad was brought from his cloth-shrinking bench that was where he decided they must go; he was never known to act against his mother's advice, except when she tried to interfere with his drinking habits.

They found me perched on a high desk in Police Headquarters, surrounded by laughing men in blue uniforms. I was clutching chocolate in both hands and my face was a brown and sticky mess. 'You'd have made a good advert for Cadbury's,' my father used to say.

Since that sunlit morning – on the stage, in films and on the television screen – I have played every rank of policeman (plain-clothes and uniformed) from the bobby on the beat up to and including the Home Secretary. It is my only claim to fame, and I like to think that some of the inspiration for it came from that friendly copper who plucked me from the arms of my rescuer, hoisted me high in the air, and then plonked me down on the saddle directly in front of him.

Thanks, constable. Between you and me, it turned out to be quite a ride ...

Chapter Three

❖

Beginners, please!

With Dad now firmly established as a cloth-finisher at John Holt and Sons ('London Dyers and Shrinkers'), money matters were somewhat easier. Decent toys could now and then be afforded, Albert and I were given a little pocket-money sometimes, and even the occasional special treat started to come our way. This was the year I was given a scooter on which I would tear madly up and down Grant Street, from Holt's mill at one end to the corner-shop at the other. 'But don't you take it down Garnett Street, *we don't want it pinched,*' Mum always warned me. My brother and I were forbidden to mix with the Garnett Street crowd because all the dwellers in Grant Street flattered themselves that the slums began at our little corner-shop and stretched down to Leeds Road on the left and up to Barkerend Road on the right, in other words the length and breadth of the infamous Garnett Street. Occasionally we would sneak 'down Garnett' on Saturday nights when Dad and Mum were out; and some of the fights and domestic squabbles we witnessed after closing-time were quite spectacular. It is a favourite subject with cartoonists, but I have actually seen a woman, in a long apron and a man's flat cap, stand in front of her house and bang her husband over the head with a frying-pan repeatedly as he stood there, drunk and incapable, and let her do it. As she beat him rhythmically and mercilessly, this termagant was chanting: 'Whoring, that's where you've been – whoring! Oo, I could bash your brains out!' And all of us kids, clustered in the yellow glow of the street-lamp at half-past ten at night, jumped up and down and applauded her madly. You always got bags of entertainment down Garnett Street, and it was free for all – in more senses than one.

I was starting to learn many things by now, officially as well as privately. Before I was five, I was enrolled as a pupil at Barkerend Infants' School on Butler Street.

Schools then were a far cry from the bright, airy and indulgent establishments of today. You, the pupil, were not supposed to enjoy any part of them, with the possible exception of the games-field. You were there to learn, and to learn hard. And if you didn't learn, you suffered. By stern disciplinary measures and the employment of teachers who knew how to administer them, you were given a thorough grounding in the three R's – reading, writing and 'rithmetic. The rest (and that included the misty possibilities of higher education which Albert was already sampling farther up the road) was up to you.

The alphabet came first of course, and then we were taught to put words together, doing our elementary reading from books of fairy-tales. When we became more literate our reading prowess was tested publicly, as one by one we were made to stand in front of the class and read aloud from such popular classics as *Coral Island* and *Black Beauty*. I was very bad at this, because for the first few years of my life I spoke with a thick lisp and that, combined with my broad Yorkshire accent, made my attempts at public speaking lamentable and almost unintelligible.

We were taught to write on slates, with slate-pencils. The screeching and squealing made by these, wielded by unskilled, babyish hands, was something indescribable, and must have caused many a sensitive junior 'Miss' to think seriously about changing her vocation. I was better at this than at the reading though, and liked it when imagination was given full rein and we were allowed to make up our own short and simple sentences.

I had scant regard for discipline then, and have hated most rules and regulations all my life; consequently, I was frequently in trouble. My class-mistress was Miss Bignall, a small and dumpy woman with frantic hair and the reddest of cheeks. But what the redoubtable Miss Bignall lacked in stature she made up for in forcefulness. She scorned the use of a cane, and had in its place the long handle of a croquet-mallet. This was made of turned wood, heavily varnished, and had along its length gaudily painted rings of red, yellow and green. My hands took many a sadistic beating from this instrument of torture, but it is more than likely that I deserved them all. Sometimes however, Miss Bignall literally laid it on too thick. At the end of one morning I went home to my dinner (we never called it 'lunch' in Yorkshire) and was so ashamed of the state of my hands that I hid them under the table and told my mother I wasn't hungry so that, hopefully, she would not catch sight of them. Because I have always liked my food, this statement took her completely by surprise; and it wasn't long before she found out the true reason for my pretended indisposition. She looked down at my red and battered hands, with their open cuts where the croquet-mallet had been more than usually vicious, and asked me how all this had come about. I couldn't claim that I'd been fighting, as all the evidence was on my palms and the insides of my fingers; there were no bruised knuckles and the backs of my hands, though grubby, were unscathed. I had to confess to her about Miss Bignall. Mum said nothing, but her face set hard.

'Right. Now you've owned up – and don't take so long about it in future – eat your dinner, and get back to school.'

I did as I was bid, fearful that the evening might bring a more severe admonition from my father when he heard about my misdeeds.

Half-way through the afternoon, when for once the classroom was completely quiet as Miss Bignall intoned to us some words of wisdom, the door was wrenched violently open and my mother stood there fuming, with a fluttering headmistress bringing up the rear. She glared at my teacher, who rose from her desk in some consternation.

'So you're Miss Bignall, are you?'

My tormentress half-nodded. Mum's glance flickered round the room, and lighted on me. In silence she crossed to pluck me from my bench, and then almost frog-marched me to the headmistress, holding out my hands to her with the palms upwards. Then she jerked me round and manhandled me across to Miss Bignall.

'Did you do that to my lad?'

'I – I – ' The poor fat lady was lost for words.

'You did, didn't you? Well, see how *you* like it!'

With a clenched fist she struck Miss Bignall full in the face, and then grabbed her and hauled her to the ground. In a second the two of them were a thumping, scratching, biting pile of flesh. My headmistress tried to separate them and was smacked across the chops for her pains; yowling, she fled the room. My mother finally staggered to her feet out of breath, her cub suitably avenged, and left her victim in a moaning and slobbering heap.

'Come on, lad.' I followed her to the door, not knowing where to look. I ran past her into the Main Hall, as she turned on them: 'And he won't be coming back until he's better!'

Nowadays I suppose there would be actions for assault and battery, court cases, fines and heavy damages. As it was, I don't think I ever heard another word about the incident – and I don't think that damned coloured stick was ever used on me again.

I learned a lot at Barkerend, and not all of it was to my advantage. There are two things about education: the first is to acquire what knowledge you can, and the second is to put it to useful application. I was fairly good at the first, but went sadly adrift sometimes on the second: you have to learn when and how to use properly what you have picked up.

And you assimilate a lot at infant school, in addition to the three R's. For one thing you extend your vocabulary, but not always in the right direction. All my life I have been keen on words that are new to me, and strive to use a recent acquisition

Mother and her young! *Photo: Author's collection*

as soon as possible, especially if it's a good, solid, well-sounding word and preferably of Anglo-Saxon origin.

I went down to breakfast in this mood one morning, and my mother placed a fried egg in front of me. Dad sat on my left with his back to the fire.

'Get it down you.'

I considered my plate with an air of self-importance. I dwelt a pause. I was now going to impress the whole family with my erudition. Especially Albert.

'Go on, lad,' Dad encouraged.

I looked first at him, then at my brother on the opposite side and finally round at my mother, who stood frowning at my delay and wiping her hands on her pinny. They fell silent, and all three were looking back at me. This was it.

'We get eggs, don't we?' I informed them loftily, 'But there's never any fucking bacon.'

My father gave me one almighty swipe. My chair went over backwards, and I shot across the floor and cracked my head on the skirting-board under the window. My mother moved towards me.

'Leave him alone, Alice; he'll get worse than that if he doesn't watch his lip from now on.'

I never again swore in front of either of my parents; not even so much as a simple 'damn'.

In 1926, my first school year, trade began to slump in Bradford and men started to be 'laid off'. My father could see the signs and portents, though his time was still some way ahead, and began to develop what was at first quite a lucrative sideline. He had a way with comic songs and monologues, and could always be relied on to come up with one or two choice items at any family gathering. I believe he had enjoyed this gift from boyhood, and it had been much encouraged by his fellow infantrymen in the trenches and estaminets, where entertainment was often hard to come by. In earlier days he had even composed his own material, together with some telling lyrics. One that sticks in my mind is a parody of an old ragtime number, *Back Home In Tennessee*, and should for full effect be sung to the same tune.

> *Way down in Oppy Wood, up to your neck in mud,*
> *Be sure it is no fun, to go and strafe the Hun;*
> *All you can think of at night is old Fritz's Very Light,*
> *Minnies dropping, machine-guns popping,*
> *All the Front's alight!*
> *The whizz-bangs as they fall, what memories they recall,*
> *You're sure to change your smile,*
> *They're dropping all the while;*
> *And then the officer will meet you,*
> *With a tot of rum he'll greet you,*
> *And he'll say 'Mate – retaliate –*
> *With a Millses Number Five!*

The Number Five of course was the famous Mills hand-grenade: scant defence against the mighty armoury of the Bosche.

Now Dad decided to help the state of the economy by turning these talents to a more productive use. At first he sang in the pubs, going round cap in hand at the end of his 'turn'. The pennies and threepenny-bits were stowed away, the cap replaced on his head and off he would go to the next hostelry down the street; and there were dozens and dozens of pubs in Bradford at that time. Soon he was known in all of them as 'Bert Sands – Comic Singer.' One or two club bookings began to filter in, and these carried a fixed fee and a good deal more prestige. And there seemed to be a working-men's club in every corner of the city. Gradually over the years, Bert Sands became a local celebrity and was at last made a life-member of the Northern Variety Artistes' Association ... but I am leaping ahead, and he still has a long way to go before club-singing becomes his only means of livelihood.

He had a cousin on his mother's side called Jack Hemmans, a postman by trade. Due to his withered arm Jack had a war disability pension and this, combined with his postman's wages, gave him a steady weekly income. But Jack was the ambitious type. He had seen famous double-acts like Layton and Johnstone, Murray and Mooney, Bennett and MacNaughton and even a struggling duo called Flanagan and Allen, at the local variety houses; and he saw no reason why Bert and he should not emulate their prowess. So Bert and Jack became *Sands and Grant*, my Uncle Jack changing his surname to that of the street where his partner lived. They worked together and singly, in offerings that ranged from the broadly comic to the unashamedly sentimental. Their double-acts they called 'stunts' and their single acts were 'specialities'.

On occasion, Albert and I were allowed to go with my mother to watch Sands and Grant as they slowly became fully-fledged entertainers, deserting the pubs and concentrating on clubs, dinners and smoking-concerts. Their bookings were usually at week-ends, and they were sometimes engaged by the same club for sessions on Saturday night, Sunday dinner-time and Sunday evening. I earned my first coppers as a performer at the age of seven, standing on a billiards-table at Bradford Moor Labour Club and singing a tune of the times called *My Little Wooden Whistle Wouldn't Whistle*.

But in 1926 much of this still lay in the future. It was the year of the General Strike, and I remember Uncle Jack helped to maintain public services by volunteering to drive a tram.

Not that the Strike meant much to Albert and me. He was busy concluding his first year at Hanson Secondary School and I was having my battles with Miss Bignall in the daytime, and playing out on the street in the evenings. There were few organised sports clubs and no youth centres, so we made our own outdoor fun in the summer, and huddled over our magic lanterns and cigarette-cards in the winter. The street games we played (apart from the perennial cricket and football) were lusty shouting-matches with a lot of running and jumping attached to them. They had colourful names like Relievo, Tin Can Squat and Piggy.

Sometimes, if you were lucky, the man in the checked sportscoat and trilby hat would come, pushing his street-organ up Garnett Street in front of him. We called him the Tingalary Man. His instrument was the size of a small upright piano. It

44

was mounted on wheels, and fitted with a pair of shafts. It had no captive monkey, though we heard these were customary down South. If there were one or two people about, chatting on their doorsteps (and a lot of that went on in those days), he would park his bulky instrument outside the corner-shop, drop his upturned hat on the cobbles and start turning the handle. The pinned and perforated discs inside would play loud and jangly tunes like *Valencia*, *Carolina Moon*, *I Do Like To Be Beside The Seaside* and (the one that always made me stop and think) the haunting *Roses of Picardy*. I would give him my last ha'penny if I had one, I loved his music so much.

In autumn, the man who sold cooked peas might come round. He was lame, and carried twin canisters swinging from a yoke round his neck, grey peas on the left and green peas on the right. His street-cry was 'Peasalot!' and I used to think this meant he would give you a lot of peas if you took him a penny and a pint pot; but experience and the mingy amounts he doled out taught me that what he was really shouting was 'Peas – all hot!' One foggy evening a stray cat, being chased by a furious dog, jumped into one of his canisters and suffered a terrible end. I wasn't present but I heard all about it, because for some days it was the talk of the neighbourhood. For some reason I could never fathom, this sad occurrence made Grant Street laugh its head off.

If all else failed, we would resort to brick-fights. There were two pet sites for this activity: the open space near the Hippodrome, which was always littered with stones and bricks; and Fatty's Yard, a derelict area behind a wooden gate next to the offices of John Holt and Sons. To one of these we would repair, usually at the invitation of a rival street-gang, and indulge in occupying rough ditches some ten yards apart and hurling bricks, stones and broken glass at each other until sufficient bruising had been incurred and enough blood had been spilt for us to call it a day. It never occurred to me then that this wasn't the only game we played that had its origin in the savagery of the Great War that had ended less than a decade before.

When we could afford it, we went to the pictures. They were silent films of course, and we usually watched them at the Hippodrome, which was within easy walking distance of our street. The programmes in those days were not continuous. In the evenings, following the manner of the live theatres, there were two performances, 'first and second house'; and on Saturday afternoons, there was the weekly glory of the 'Tupp'ny Rush'. This was when the Garnett Street Gang always turned out in force, and you could rarely watch the show through without noisy outbreaks of yelling and brawling – so Albert and I strove to avoid it ...

Regular occurrence, wasn't it, Les? Friday night at the Hippo – provided we could raise the cash. I remember one Friday in particular, somewhere around the time of the General Strike. I'd be – what? – I'd be ten or eleven. There was this cowboy picture on that we both wanted to see; Buck Jones I believe it was, or maybe Hoot Gibson. And we were skint, as usual. I think it cost us fourpence each at that time – half-price of course – so what we wanted was eightpence between us. That 'ud be less than four new pence in Mickey Mouse money. And I couldn't raise the coppers anyhow. I knew if I went to see Grandma Riley at Friday teatime I'd get tuppence, because I used to go shopping in Leeds Road for Grandma Riley and it was always a regular tuppence. But obviously that wouldn't be sufficient. I tried to think of all ways. And then it struck me, once or twice Grandma Sands had asked me to take some rags on to Medley's, in Pit Lane. She'd always given me a penny to the shilling on those rags. So I went round there and said, 'I just wondered, Grandma, have you got any rags I can take to Medley's for you?' 'Oh,' she said, 'I don't think so. Why?' I said, 'Well, I just want to make a copper or two for me and our Les to go to the Hippodrome tonight.' 'Aw, I see.' She was hard was Grandma Sands you know, but she had a soft heart. 'Come back in an hour,' she said, 'and I'll see what I can put together.' Well, time was getting on!

And you kept jumping up and down and saying 'Are we going then, Alb – are we going?' You always loved cowboy pictures. I said, 'We'll have to wait and see.' Eventually I got back round there and, 'Ah,' says my grandma, 'I've got some – but there isn't all that many, like.' My heart sank. But she gave me the sack – and I don't think there was a shillingsworth of rags really, but at least it was something. So we set off, me with this sack over my shoulder, on Pit Lane. About three-quarters of the way along, there's a pony-and-cart coming towards us, obviously coming from the rag-and-bone yard. This fellow pulls up. 'Where you off to with that sack, lad?' 'Medley's. They're rags.' 'Nay, don't bother going that far,' he says, 'I'll buy 'em off you.' I said: 'You won't, you know – these are going where they belong.' 'You'll only get tuppence or threepence there,' he says, but I said, 'Gerraway! I'll get a shilling at least.' I knew I wouldn't, but I wasn't going to let on. 'Tell you what,' he says, 'I'll give you eightpence.' I said, 'No, no. I'll get a bob out of old Medley.' He said, 'Go on, then, *tenpence*.' I considered, and then: 'All right,' I says, and I put 'em on his flat cart. He gave me tenpence. 'Now then,' I thought, 'I've got tenpence – but I don't know whether I'll even get a penny out of Grandma Sands on that,' and my heart dropped into my boots again. And you and me, we're walking back to my grandma's and it's getting dark; not much, but a bit bluey-dark. Now as you know, there were loads of ponies-and-carts came on Pit Lane at that time, so there were piles of muck all over the place. We're mogging on, and I caught sight of this little pile of manure. And I saw something glint. This is true, Les – *it glinted at me.* I went over to it and moved it with my foot. It was a sixpence. I carefully picked this sixpence out. Then, being a Sands, I thought 'I wonder if there's any more?' And I shifted the stuff about again with my foot. And what d'you think – I found another tuppence. That was eightpence! So I put that in a separate pocket, and we went back to the shop in Barkerend Road. I gave Grandma Sands the tenpence for the rags and I told her the story. 'You were lucky,' she says, 'You wouldn't have got above sixpence, on at Medley's.' 'I know, Grandma.' Then she studied for a bit. 'Nah then!' she says, 'You know I generally give you a penny to the shilling?' And I nodded. 'Well this time I'm going to give you tuppence,' she says. 'Tuppence! 'Cos you acted right in your head there.' And that's what she gave me – tuppence. So I had the eightpence that I'd found in the muck, and I had my tuppence that Grandma Sands gave me *and* I had the tuppence eventually that I got from Grandma Riley, for dashing down into Leeds Road for her at the last minute. That was a SHILLING. And we went to the pictures that night in style, lad. We had two fourpennies in the pictures – and we had some sweets as well. I think we had a whole four ounces of sweets between us, just the two of us. I'll always remember that, lad – it seems like only yesterday.

I was hungry for stories now. Stories of all kinds. Stories from the films. Picture-stories from my comics like *Film Fun*, *Puck* and *The Funny Wonder*. And stories from real life, wherever they could be found.

Best of all were my father's stories. It didn't matter whether he was regaling you with a joke he had just invented, or slowly detailing (and he had to be persuaded into this) some of his exploits in the Great War. 'Tell us a war-tale, Dad,' I would beg him, whenever I could get him on his own.

He told me of frightening things, like the murderous crossfire from machine-guns and the yellow drift of mustard gas across the wastes of no-man's land. In one attack he jumped down into a German front line which had been largely evacuated, and charged into an enemy dug-out with a captured revolver at the ready. A young German in field-grey

Sergeant Sands.

Photo: Author's collection

was huddled, petrified, against the opposite wall, his rifle on the floor at his feet. As my father entered he pulled a photograph from his breast-pocket and held it out in silent supplication. It showed his flaxen-haired wife and their young son. My father took pity on him and jerked his head towards the open air. The man fled, and my father went on to search an inner compartment. Something made him turn – to see the reprieved German boy coming back towards him with a bayonet in his fist and grinning all over his face.

'I shot him dead, Les, on the spot. And then I kicked his face in, for being what he was.'

He told me only once of how he had won his mention in despatches. It happened at a time when the Allies had been bogged down for weeks in the filth and slime of the Western Front, with rats and lice as their constant companions. Information came that the Germans were to launch a heavy barrage at dawn. Just before morning light, it was realised that a machine-gun nest out in the wasteland had not been ordered to retire, due to a breakdown in communications. Volunteers were requested to go out and help them back. No-one was willing to risk being caught out there at dawn in the shot and shell, until my dad took one pace forward. '568 Sergeant Sands, sir!' He was issued with a pouch of hand-grenades and his comrades wished him luck. Then it was over the top, through the barbed wire, and a long crawl on his belly across no-man's land.

When he reached the emplacement it had three occupants, all of whom had enlisted with him. One man was dead, another badly wounded and the third fainting from terror and exposure. My father immobilised the Lewis gun, dumped all his heavy gear (for which he was later castigated), took the wounded soldier across his back and, with the man who could still walk clinging to him for support, began the long and perilous trek back to the front line. When he staggered down into the trench, the man on his back was dead too. The officer shook him by the hand, and gave him a measure of rum.

And then the officer will meet you,
With a tot of rum he'll greet you,

And he'll say 'Mate – retaliate –
With a Millses Number Five!'

His certificate is in front of me as I write.

"West Yorkshire Regiment No. 16/568 Serjt. A.E. Sands, 16th Battalion, was mentioned in a Despatch from Field Marshal Sir Douglas Haig GCB, GCVO, KCIE, dated 9th April 1917 for gallant and distinguished services in the Field. I have it in command from the King to record His Majesty's high appreciation of the services rendered."

It is signed in black ink, 'Winston S. Churchill', who at that time was the Secretary of State for War.

That year of the General Strike also saw my first stumbling attempt at straight acting. It was during the end-of-term party at Barkerend Infants, and I played the name part in a teacher's adaptation of *Rumpelstiltskin*. I was inordinately proud of my costume, made out of green and orange crêpe paper, and I showed off shamelessly in performance to the assembled crowd of somewhat bored infants. I would learn eventually, as Stanislavsky learned before me, that in acting you must love the art in yourself and not yourself in the art. But these were early days.

Dad was still in work then and twice, in 1926 and 1927, we went on holiday to Blackpool. On each occasion we travelled by charabanc. The first Blackpool trip was literally a wash-out, because the charabanc's removable cover wasn't working, and it rained very heavily. What's more, the downpour continued for our whole week there. The second visit was a great success. We had lodgings in Charnley Road, and Albert and I would sally forth on sunny, carefree mornings, sometimes separately but nearly always together, to sniff the salt breezes and sample the delights of sea and beach, the spectacular piers and the innumerable arcades and amusement-parks. We were both bought ukuleles on this visit. Albert got himself an instruction-manual, and was soon strumming away as to the manner born. He taught me a few elementary chords and we raised the roof at the lodgings playing and singing *Ukulele Lady*, *Piccolo Pete*, *Drifting and Dreaming* and the like.

At the boarding-house was another local family who hailed from Wingfield Street, where I would in years to come deliver newspapers. They had a daughter of about my age, and on one glorious day we donned our bathing-suits and went paddling together. This somewhat forward young miss invited me into their room when we returned. Her parents were out with mine, she wanted to rinse the sand off her legs and feet, and wondered if I would care to dry them for her? I accepted with alacrity and couldn't grab the towel quickly enough, once she was busy with jug and basin at the wash-hand-stand. Afterwards, as she lay on top of the patchwork quilt in her skimpy, sap-green swimming costume, I tried to put my arms round her. But this, the first 'tease' I ever came across, would have none of it.

'No, I'm thirsty. Let's have a drink of water,' and she scrambled off the bed and over to the jug again. There was a handy glass and she filled it, evidently thinking something over. 'Tell you what,' she said, 'we'll have some of this in it!' And she liberally laced the unoffending liquid with two large spoonfuls of Andrews' Liver Salts. We knocked the whole lot back together.

I don't know how she got on later, but I had quite a busy afternoon in the upstairs bathroom.

After our return home I told Grandma Sands about our holiday, carefully omitting any reference to the young lady from Wingfield Street. She cautioned me against too much frivolity and money-spending.

'Save your coppers, lad, and concentrate on your schooling; that'll get you a lot further than holidays.' She would always be my counsellor and friend, though her manner was strict and forbidding and her outlook on life usually more than glum.

Grandma Sands.

Photo: Author's collection

Her sayings and precepts, though sometimes difficult for a young mind to encompass immediately, were invariably shrewd and pithy.

'Speak the truth and shame the devil.'

'Never be poor and look poor.'

'Always try and mix with somebody a bit better than you are – better placed, better educated or more talented. And when you can equal them, mix with somebody a bit better still.'

'If you mix wi' muck, you'll stink.'

'Before doing a thing, always study well what the end may be.'

'Make sure you have enough money for your needs – and never enough for your wants.'

'Never forget, a boy's greatest ambition is to be a man; and a man's greatest ambition is to be a boy.'

'There's no such thing as luck: the harder you work, the luckier you'll get.'

Words to live by, Grandma. And I did my best – honestly.

Albert was ploughing on manfully at the secondary school, going his own way with his customary quiet determination. At home he always passed on new-found knowledge to me, as if he wanted me to keep in step with him. At bedtime, up in the little room with the institution green walls, I had my first lessons in French and Spanish. Absolute mysteries like algebra and geometry were mentioned and – much later on – something quite fantastic that only elder brothers could understand, called 'trigonometry'. Long after we'd blown the candle out we would lie side by side, singing the songs he was learning at school. *Shenandoah* was my top favourite because we could harmonise with that one; that is, Albert could do the harmony, while I coped with the basic air. Sometimes, just as we were dropping off to sleep, there would come a tickling and an itching and we would have to light the candle, get out of bed and deal with the bugs.

A bedbug is a small, roundish, fascinating creature, that seems to glow with a purple incandescence when it has recently fed off human blood. They were in the walls and woodwork at Grant Street, and always waited until you were warm and cosy before they came out to mount an attack. The subsequent itching could drive you frantic. No matter what we did, the bugs always seemed to be with us. Some people say they can smell bugs, just as they can smell the presence of mice. I never had this questionable proficiency, but I was a dab-hand at squeezing them sharply to death. Their pathetic remains and the blood they had gorged on would be sticky on your fingers, and you would wipe these clean on your night-time shirt; we never wore pyjamas, because you only enjoyed that life-style if you had to go into hospital. My father found a fairly good remedy was to move the bed away from the wall and stand its legs in little tins of paraffin. For a while this had its effect – but they always came back. Our Alb used to say, 'You can't keep a good bedbug down.'

Around this time my mother took me on my one and only visit to the mill. I think she must have been seeking work, because I was left on a greasy bench while she went over and had a lengthy conversation with a huge man in a great blue-and-white checked overall. He was something called an 'overlooker' in the weaving-shed, and seemed to be tremendously important. After that we walked through all the various departments and I watched the washing, the combing, the spinning and the weaving, all in turn. I hated everything about the place, the flagged yard where mill-lads always seemed to be playing football, the oily floors and dirty ceilings, the lack of light, the bawdy conversation of the mill-lasses, the conscious superiority of the foremen and overlookers, the unique smell of sweat, steam and raw, unprocessed wool and – most of all – the deafening clacking of the looms. This was a world of its own; and it was a world I desperately hoped I would be able to avoid.

Some years, when she felt up to it, Grandma Sands would give one of her great Christmas parties. Attendance was obligatory at these for all the Sandses, now a numerous roll-call thanks to her eight fertile children and their wives and husbands. A week or so before Christmas itself came along, every Sands who could walk or be carried would forgather at her command in the living-room at 194 at six o'clock in the evening. The men had finished work by then, and there had just been time for them to change into dark suits and high stiff-collars. First we would be regaled with the most enormous high tea. Great mounds of ham salad would be carried through by the daughters, who had been in the kitchen all afternoon, busily preparing. There would be two or three mouth-watering 'stand-pies' (so called because they were large and heavy enough to require a cake-stand to support them) cut into man-sized wedges; tinned salmon and cucumber for those who had no liking for meat; sausages, pork, beef and pork-and-beef, cut in halves and more than a little charred on the outsides; dishes of hard-boiled eggs; a plethora of plates of cold roast beef and pork; and everywhere, slices of bread and margarine. I don't remember any chicken-legs or turkey drumsticks, but then poultry was an expensive luxury in those days. Tomato ketchup had not yet come into favour in the North, but piccalilli and the thick and juicy H.P. sauce were well in evidence; and home-pickled onions were there in profusion of course, in a towering glass jar. From the shop that sold hot food next door (run, incidentally, by the only woman I ever knew called Leah) huge canteen teapots had been borrowed, and were put to good and constant use by the thirty or forty Sandses gathered together in family harmony. After you had stuffed yourself to bursting-point with all these unaccustomed savoury delights, huge glass dishes of tinned peaches, pears and apricots would appear, accompanied by jugs of Carnation Milk, a cream substitute that turned every sweet it covered into ambrosia.

Then we would all lumber our way upstairs to Grandma's best room, the drawing-room. This was above the shop itself, and had not only an immense, white marble fireplace covered in her china seaside souvenirs, but also sofas, leather and velvet-covered, chairs that enveloped you like a long-lost aunt, and a real pile-carpet. It even featured an upright piano in teak, that had always been specially tuned for the great occasion. In this regal chamber, beer and stout would be dispensed to the adults, while still lemonade, pop, sarsaparilla or a delicious drink called 'dandelion-and-burdock' were ladled out in great draughts to the young ones. Now came the high-spot of the evening, the Family Concert. Uncle Percy (Percy North, my godfather and husband to my favourite auntie, Ethel) would fling off his blue-serge jacket, roll up his striped shirt-sleeves, seat himself with much adjustment on the revolving piano stool and, after one great, resounding chord, the evening's entertainment would commence.

Everyone without exception had to 'give a turn'; and Grandma Sands presided over all, magnificent in a long, black silk dress with strings of chunky beads round her chubby neck and shoulders. Dad was naturally the star with his comic songs, some of them specially written for him by G.P. Logan, a resident pianist at one of Bradford's finest clubs.

Why does the missis want to row with me?
What's the reason we
Can never agree?
She's nag, nag, nagging, all day long;
She's always right, and I'm always wrong.
The other night I hit her with a bottle and she sighed,
When I saw what I'd done lads, you can bet I nearly died,
The bottle that I hit her with had Tetley's Best inside!
Why does the missis want to row with me?

My mother always rendered one of her sentimental ballads, to Uncle Percy's somewhat erratic but enthusiastic accompaniment. It might be *Love's Old Sweet Song*, *The Farmer's Boy* or perhaps *The Old Tramp*. She had many others in her repertoire but some were so sad that Albert would beg her before we set off not to sing them, because they reduced him to tears and that made him feel a fool. Her voice – and I can hear it now, spanning all the years – was sweet and true:

You may laugh, you may chaff
Because I am down in the world,
But you'll find out to your sorrow

57

> *You're up today and down tomorrow:*
> *Never make mock of misfortune,*
> *For what has to be will be;*
> *I might have been up in the world like you,*
> *And you might have been down like me.*

Albert himself had his tried and trusted monologues, *The Little Crossing-Sweeper* being the most-requested item; and I would usually deliver some poem I had recently learned at school, holding my head up as my dad had taught me, keeping my hands still and projecting with all my might and main. 'Let 'em have it at the back,' he always dinned into me.

And so the evening would roll on in fun and laughter and not without a few well-placed tears, as the men got tipsier and tipsier, and the ladies, mellowed by glasses of Guinness with foaming tops, grew more and more sentimental and reminiscent in their tight little groups.

Cousin Eddie, the only child of Uncle Percy and Aunt Ethel, would weigh in with a dependable little ditty that went something like this:

> *Five little fags in a dainty little packet,*
> *Five cigarettes that cost two-dee,*
> *Five little pains underneath his jacket,*
> *Five little wobbles in his little Mary:*
> *Five little whiffs*
> *And in five little jiffs*
> *You'll see Willie on the tramway lines;*
> *And underneath his jacket*
> *There'll be found a little packet*
> *That contains four Wild Woodbines!*

The end of the concert followed a familiar pattern, and the last three items were nearly always the same. Grandad Sands, far removed now from his Worcestershire fields and farms, his cobbler's leather apron discarded on his bench downstairs, would render:

So give me a nail and a hammer
And a picture to hang on the wall,
A ladder – and someone to hold it –
And a cushion in case I should fall;
With two boys to bring in the bevvy
Plus a doctor, if I should turn pale,
And I'll bet I'll hang up that picture –
If somebody knocks in the nail!

His eldest child Ethel would then offer a rendition of *There's A Long, Long Trail A-Winding*; and her eyes would go dewy as she thought back a few years, to when her Percy and those of her brothers who were old enough to serve had all been in khaki.

But Percy North would never let the night end on a sad note. Beered up now, and with his wispy ginger hair flying wild, Percy would hammer on the yellowed keys without a care in the world and bawl out, solo, the last rousing chorus of the evening:

Onward, onward to the top of the hill,
Looking for a flowerpot on a window-sill;
Happy and gay, singing all the way,
Yip-aye, yip-aye, addy-aye-ay –
Rolling, strolling, bowling along,
Says to his wifey at the door:
'Here's the black sheep of the family,
Back to the fold once more!'

He would give a flourishing roll right up the keyboard from deepest bass to highest treble, and then conclude with a final triumphant and thunderous chord ... and that was it.

It would be between ten and eleven o'clock, and back we would all go to our individual folds joyously, to talk about that marvellous meal and the matchless entertainment – and to hope it wouldn't be too long before that old piano was tuned up to concert pitch again.

Chapter Four

❖

Twenty Past Eight

'Go on – you'll like it at your grandma's –'

'I won't,' I said sulkily.

'It's only for a couple of days, anyway.' My mother sounded unusually stern, for her. I noticed her breathing was laboured. She seemed to have put on weight lately.

'You said –'

'Here's your carrier. Now blow your nose and get on up there. Think on, be a good lad.'

It was February 1928, and for some unknown reason I was being bundled off on my own away from Grant Street.

My mother's parents, Grandma and Grandad Riley, lived in Seaton Street, half a mile away from us. But being farther up the hill and out of Bradford's centre, Seaton Street was looked upon as a rather more salubrious area. It was superior to both Grant and Garnett Streets in that it had clean and at that time unbroken flagstones and cobbles, two general stores and a fish-and-chip shop of its very own. Grandma and Grandad lived near the bottom, again up a passage, in one of the houses at the back. But this passage was flagged – there were even windows in it that looked out of real kitchens – and the two houses in their little yard had their own squares of garden, which you had to cross to get to the outside toilets. Grandma Riley's patch was always a mass of flowers; she had a great fondness for scarlet and gold antirrhinums and the fragile beauty of canterbury bells.

The house was spotless and, in addition to the downstairs living-room, had a long kitchen that was twice the size at least of our little scullery at home. The upstairs accommodation also outclassed ours, for at Seaton Street they had three bedrooms, one big, one medium and one small. The Rileys had a lodger called Phil, who specialised in the making of crystal-sets. Real wireless-sets were coming on the market now, but they were as yet few and far between in the land of the back-to-backs.

Grandad Riley was a tall, spare man who never seemed quite certain of keeping his balance and who, even in middle age, had a blue skin over one of his eyeballs which must have been a cataract and gave him a rather sinister aspect. Grandma Riley, on the other hand, was an apple dumpling of a woman, small and rounded, who wore a snowy pinafore and always looked newly scrubbed. There wasn't an ounce of harm in her, she spoiled her grandchildren beyond redemption, and always smelled of the white windsor soap that graced the stone sink and the copper in her kitchen. This last was for boiling clothes on washing-day, and that was always Monday. The clothes were then rinsed and mangled before being hung up to dry on a washing-line across the garden in summer, and crowded on wooden clothes-horses round the fire in winter. Grandma always called a clothes-horse a 'winter-edge' and it was years and years before I learned that country people would set their household linen out to dry on hedges in the summer, but in the harsher seasons would have to use an indoor help of this sort; in other words, a *winter-hedge*. Grandad too had a colourful turn of phrase, using dialect words that now seem to have vanished from our ken due to the spread of popular education, the dissemination of B.B.C. English and the unstemmable influence of the other media. He always called his broad braces 'gallusses' and again it took me a long time to realise this was a corruption of 'gallows', another highly efficient means of suspension. He never 'went' anywhere; he always 'gat agate': and he was never 'going to' do something, he was always 'bahn tull'.

On a frosty Wednesday that February I was sent up to their house to stay three nights, until the Saturday morning; and, incomprehensibly, this visit might be extended if word to that effect should come from home. I had no idea at all of what lay behind all this but went off happily enough after school on Wednesday, with spare shirt, singlet, socks and hanky in the inevitable brown carrier-bag. Grandad was his usual unapproachable self, and would sit in the evenings crouched over the paper for hours, devouring it with the aid of a large, black-framed magnifying glass. Grandma was busy with her chores, but found time to tell me stories of the mill and to read to me from the few books they had on a shelf in the corner. Phil the lodger made much of me, took me out for walks and encouraged me to listen to his wireless. At night, owing to there being only two beds in the house and one of them in the middle room for Phil, I slept between my maternal grand-parents in their seemingly gigantic double bed in the large room. I remember Grandad snored like a traction-engine, Grandma twitched and murmured in her sleep, and the pillows and sheets had an acrid smell due to the pipe-smoking to which Grandad Riley was incurably addicted. He smoked thick twist and its odour permeated the entire house, apart from the kitchen. There was a good reason for this. He was of the old school, who believed that woman's place was strictly in the home and that man must never lift a finger to help her; consequently there was never any tobacco-smoke in the kitchen, where the aroma of white windsor soap reigned supreme. My grandma was an excellent cook, and one of her specialities was creamy rice-pudding with a thick skin on top stained brown with nutmeg. She knew my predilection for this dish, and I was presented with it once a day during my short visit with a regular top-up in the evenings.

On the Saturday morning, by which time the sun had broken through and dispelled the last of the frost, I was sent back home and, having been a 'good lad' in accordance with my mother's instructions, was given a penny for 'spice'. There was a little sweet-shop at the bottom, round the corner in Browning Street, and I bought two ounces of Maynard's wine gums and munched my way happily back to Grant Street. I pushed the door open and marched into the living-room where, to my surprise, I found the brass bedstead had been brought down from upstairs and plonked under the window. In it was my mother, looking tired but the picture of contentment. Lying next to her and suckling at her breast was a complete stranger. He was tiny, and had a wrinkled red face.

'Nah then, Les. This is your brother Bill.'

William Henry Sands, my junior by almost seven years, had arrived upon the scene.

Unlike many cases I have heard of, I felt no resentment at his intrusion, nor was I sad at being no longer the baby of the family; but I think somebody might have told me he was coming.

Grandma Sands of course had her usual caustic comment at the ready: 'Now your nose'll be out of joint – you wait and see.'

That September, while Bill was keeping us all awake at nights, I started at Hanson Junior School. This nestled in the shadow of the mighty Hanson Seniors, up Barkerend Road. My first teacher here was the soft-voiced and spectacled Miss Leadley, who was followed by Miss Rawson, a cheery chatter-box of a woman more given to telling us tales than to teaching us properly. The class numbered about forty and I stayed with the same group during Standards One, Two, Three and Four, responding in various degrees to the tutelage of the Misses Leadley, Rawson and, for the final two years, Miss Dickinson. This last was an inspired teacher who taught us joined-up writing, the proper application of our primitive mathematics, an appreciation of art, and a love of decent literature.

Miss Leadley though was the mild and understanding one. She it was who introduced us to our multiplication tables and to Christina G. Rossetti; and it was she who taught us the names of flowers. I try even to this day to have a vase of her favourite blooms in the house whenever I can, the gaudy, orangey-red chinese lanterns displaying themselves shame-lessly against a background of the silvery pureness of honesty.

Half a century later, when I was appearing at the National Theatre in the late seventies, I had a letter from Miss Leadley recalling our association and wishing me well. She must have been a septuagenarian by then and her neatly formed handwriting was as always immaculate.

While I was still in her class in Standard One, I returned home one Friday evening – famished as usual – to find my mother standing by the table with a face as white as her pinny and eyes that were large, red-rimmed, and darker than I had ever seen them. Dad sat at the table near her and she had one arm round his slumped shoulders. His own arms were stretched out in front of him and he was resting his head on them, face-down. It was clear that something terrible had happened.

'What's up? Dad? Mother?' There was no reply. 'Is it our Bill – summat wrong?' But Bill was sleeping peacefully in his pram, anchored near the low cupboard. My heart constricted in the continuing silence. 'It's not our Alb?' There was no sign of my elder brother – but then, school finished later for him, at a quarter past four.

'No, it's your dad.' My mother's voice was flat and hopeless. 'He's been laid off at Holt's. He's out o' work.'

It was the beginning of seven long years of unemployment for my father. And the Slump, which seemed to grow worse and worse with every passing year, would have grave consequences for us all.

But at the start of it, it didn't seem too onerous to me. We had nothing to spare for luxuries like football-boots or tennis-racquets, school dinners, or those little half-pint bottles of milk that cost a halfpenny each. There wouldn't be any regular pocket-money from now on, but there were always ways of scraping a few coppers together if you were willing to work at it. Dad was on the dole (for a time, at least) but he had his singing jobs to help out; so at this stage we were far from destitute. And he was with us for much more of the time, especially during the days; that, in the beginning, was a bonus.

In school holidays we would go for long walks round the town, when Dad had to go down and sign on. I was allowed

Nelson Street Labour Exchange.   *Photo: Paul Ferguson*

inside the Labour Exchange only once, and it had such an
effect on me that ever afterwards I would stand outside on the
pavement waiting for him, while he collected the few shillings
that were his due for having 'paid his stamps.' But every time
we went to the 'Labour', in the centre of a Bradford that
seemed to be growing blacker and more despondent by the
week, there were more and more men queueing up as they
waited to get in; and it took Dad longer and longer to draw his
dole, as he stood in the packed lines and shuffled ever more
slowly towards the cash-desks inside. Most of the men wore
old clothes that got more and more decrepit as time went by,
without any chance of replacement: many of them had
mufflers wound round their necks, with the ends stuffed
carelessly into their waistcoats or pullovers; and nearly all of
them wore cloth caps, not the neat and utilitarian sporting
versions we know today but great floppy caps usually made
out of boldly patterned tweed, though you did occasionally see
a gabardine or a corduroy among them. My father liked his
cap, but always wore a collar and tie in place of the customary
muffler or scarf. There was something in his nature that made
him cling, even in his darkest days, to standards of cleanliness
and respectability.

Kirkgate Market, c.1930.   *Photo: Bradford Telegraph & Argus*

We were walking along Kirkgate one day, to ascend its rise
to the well-loved Kirkgate Market. This was a vast, glass-
roofed emporium, with wrought-iron entrance-gates and wide
stone steps leading up to the dozens and dozens of stalls

within, at which you could buy anything from a length of curtain material to an elephant's foot. Everything was here, and all of it was reasonably priced. On these regular excursions we often used to visit it for a walk-round, mainly because it was warmer in there than outside, with the free heat of crowded humanity.

On our way we had to pass the Talbot Hotel. This was one of the centre's most respected hostelries, where yearly reunions used to be held for what remained of the Bradford Pals. It had a small portico of blackened stone. On the roof of this was the statue of a great mastiff dog not unlike Keeper, the one once owned by Emily Brontë. It was massive. Its haunches were firm and defiant, and its head thrust forward in truculent challenge. I always had to look up and admire it when we passed, and on this particular day my father stopped and looked up with me. He cocked his head on one side, a habit of his whenever he was focussing his attention.

'See that dog, Les? I'll tell you summat about him. Do you know, every time that dog hears the Town Hall clock strike midnight, it jumps down off that pedestal, has a run round Forster Square and then jumps up again.'

I gazed at him, wide-eyed. 'It never does!'

Dad nodded, solemn as a judge. 'It listens – look at it! – and every time it hears twelve midnight strike, down it comes.'

'But – '

'That's a fact.'

You couldn't argue with him. Not that I wanted to. I believed him without question, for my dad would never tell me a lie. With a perfectly straight face he led me on to Kirkgate Market. I accepted the legend for years. But then, I had never been in Forster Square as late as midnight. Not so far. But one day, I promised myself, when I was grown up, one day I'd be there ... and watching.

In 1929 Ramsay Macdonald became Britain's Prime Minister, after five years of Conservative rule. Labour hearts in Bradford swelled with pride and expectation. There were many thousands of these, on account of its mainly working-class population. Indeed, hadn't Bradford itself given birth to the I.L.P. back in 1893, under the astute guidance of Keir Hardie? Now Labour was back in, so the Slump couldn't possibly go on for long. How little we knew.

But battling now with the intricacies of addition, subtraction, multiplication and long division (with fractions and decimals still to come), I had little knowledge of and even less interest in the machinations of politics. There was more than enough to do, scribbling calculations in cheap 'jotters', learning Wordsworth's *Daffodils* and struggling with the mysteries of English composition. And in the evenings, while staunch Labour souls, milk-and-water Liberals and unrepentant Conservatives went off to their various clubs, there was playing-out to be protracted to the very last minute in the streets, cigarette-cards to be begged and hoarded and lurid comics to be swopped.

When Barkerend Road was cool and misty-dark, we all had our mill-band. This was a stout cord, impregnated with oil and grease, that was used for multifarious purposes in the mill. Every Bradford lad will remember mill-band, for we all carried a short length of it in our pockets when we were young. It had many uses for us, too. When the weather was frigid you lit the end of your bit and it would act as a lighted wick for hours, burning steadily and slowly, a true friend in the ice and snow. I remember cupping my palms round the glowing tip and thus warming my hands to make them ready for the next brick-fight. For elementary smokers it was a cigarette-lighter that never failed, even when the strongest winds were blowing. And I have seen Barkerend Road, blanketed in November fog, transformed into a fairyland of glow-worms as the lads came racing down its shrouded pavements whirling and twirling their mill-band into fantastic shapes and patterns of dancing red lights.

Locally, the sound of the evening mill-buzzer always spelled the end of playing-out time. This was a powerful siren, housed somewhere in Barkerend Mills. It went off at eight-twenty p.m. precisely, winter and summer, to warn the night-shift that they had ten minutes only to wait for their meal-break. We knew it as 'The Twenty Past Eight', and woe betide you if you weren't safely back in 11 Grant Street by half-past, for your supper of hot Oxo and a wedge of bread.

On Tuesday nights, if I was hungry, I would go down to the Band of Hope. This over-zealous organisation held its weekly meetings in the grimmest and gloomiest of basement-halls, along Peckover Street. Here I listened to stern lectures on moral standards, watched displays of lantern-slides usually depicting the evils of drunkenness and loose-living, goggled at wax models of diseased organs and ruined livers, and signed the pledge about once every three months. Judging by the heart-lowering exhibitions I witnessed there, there was precious little Hope for anyone in our little Band; but at least you could always be sure of getting a mug of strong, unsweetened tea and a few biscuits before you were sent on your way by your well-intentioned and undoubtedly teetotal benefactors.

I was a very healthy child, and suffered rarely from illness; though I was smitten with measles three times, which I have been told is something of a record. But I was very accident-prone, and this I suppose adjusts the balance. One or two of my accidents were indeed quite memorable.

I was at home one evening and preparing myself for bed. Mother was already upstairs, having retired early with a severe cold. She had taken my brother Bill up with her. Albert was sitting at the table with his back to the fire doing his homework, a task he always attended to with the utmost conscientiousness. On the fire itself was a large, black, cast-iron saucepan full of boiling onions, which Grandma Sands had recommended as a cure for my mother's indisposition. Dad was in for once, because of his wife's temporary incapacity; with much dark muttering, he was busy with household chores. I took my jersey off and rolled up my shirt-sleeves ready for the bedtime washing of hands and face. Crossing to the grate, I picked up the ladling-can and lifted the lid of the boiler. The usual grey mass of hot water was foaming away inside. Just as I reached over to fill the can, the coals of the fire shunted and the huge pan tumbled from the grate. Boiling water came gushing through the fireguard towards me as onions and pan fell with an almighty clatter on the hearth-tin below.

I leaped back instinctively, but hit the rear of Albert's chair. I could not escape, as the steaming liquid hissed through the wire-netting of the fireguard and covered both my legs. Screaming, I ran to the back of the house to get as far away from the fire as possible. I flung myself down on the sofa. I was in short pants still, and both my legs seemed to have gone molten. I yanked down the cycle-stockings I wore in a frenzy, to let cool air get to the shins and calves beneath. As the woolly socks went down to my ankles, the skin of my lower legs came off with them. I have never known such agony, and I hope I never shall again.

While Dad tried to comfort me, Albert was sent haring round to Grandma's to get some oil – any kind of oil – because in those days oil was believed to be the cure-all for burns and scalds. He was back in no time, gasping for breath, with a large medicine-bottle full of a greeny-grey, viscous substance known as 'carron oil', which was thick and difficult to dispense and had a stench that was vile. This was smeared liberally all over the extensive scald patches, and pink lint was applied above them. Then I was carried up to bed.

Through the days that followed, I lay there and watched my legs, as the lint grew soiled and the pain gradually became less intense and resolved itself into a dull and constant ache. My right leg had been more badly affected than the left and had four large, oblong pieces of lint glued to it, whereas the other had only two. Large blisters formed underneath these patches and began to give my parents much concern. Grandma Sands sent them to a herbalist, two doors away from her own shop. In those days there was no Health Service, and proper doctors' fees were quite beyond our means. 'I'll go and see what Mrs Watson has to say,' my dad told me. 'Grandma Sands trusts her; she's never been known to fail.'

The trustworthy Mrs Watson, to my great relief, told him that the pieces of lint must not be removed. By now all traces of the carron oil had disappeared, and the six pieces of lint were firmly cemented into my blistered flesh. 'Blisters'll burst underneath, don't you fret,' she consoled my worried parents, 'then all that badness'll go away, pass clean out through the system.' So the large and by now filthy pink oblongs remained firmly embedded in my flesh.

Part of her prophecy was correct and the huge blisters did in fact burst, eventually. But my system turned out to be uncooperative. Instead of disappearing as promised, the 'badness' stayed where it was for a long time, and then came out on the backs of my lower limbs in the form of yellow and crimson boils. My legs were going rotten.

Because of the difficulty of transporting me up and down the narrow stairs, a temporary bed had been rigged up for me under the window in the living-room. Here, to take my mind off my troubles, Dad played games with me, told me war-tales and somehow, despite his very limited means, got me comics and books to read. And so it was that I came to know Billy Bunter. The early Greyfriars yarns were becoming all the rage with the younger end. Not only did they appear in the weekly boys' magazine *The Magnet* but short novels, paperbacked, were on sale for threepence or fourpence each. In some way Dad acquired a great bundle of these from someone better off than we were, and I worked my way through them one by one, trying to understand how some boys could be sent away to live at school during term-time and had enviable things like dormitories, people called 'Matron', and rooms to work in that were known as 'studies'. During that six weeks or so of disablement, Harry Wharton and Company became my closest friends. Hot on their heels came Dixon Hawke, a fictional detective who now seems to have vanished in the mists of time and was, as it later dawned on me, a cheap copy of Sherlock Holmes.

One day Dad counted up nearly thirty boils on the back of my right leg. 'Bugger Mrs Watson!' he declared, 'It's time we had a doctor to this lad.' So a doctor was duly summoned.

I don't remember who he was or what he looked like, but was horrified when he pronounced me 'a job for the hospital'.

72

I had never been in hospital, so my heart quailed at the prospect; and I begged my parents to be spared. The doctor was adamant: one of my legs was very badly infected, and gangrene would be the next development. Unless all the lint came off soon I might well lose one limb, and it might well be two. He refused to try and remove the offensive material himself, as that operation must be done under anaesthetic and in the proper hygienic conditions.

'How much will it cost?' my mother asked. The doctor shrugged. 'You can't put a price on a leg.'

After he had gone, pocketing his fee of three-and-sixpence – which would leave us a bit short on the food front for a good few days – my dad told me we should bow to the inevitable.

'They know better than us, lad. They've studied. I'll have to make some arrangements.'

'I don't want to go, Dad!' I cried back at him.

'You can't lose your legs, love,' my mother pleaded.

'He's not going to.' Dad's voice was soft but resolute. 'And he's not going into any hospital, neither.'

'But what are we going to do, Albert?'

'We're going to get that bloody stuff off – the two of us.'

They got clean cloths and, for some reason I could not fathom, all the milk they could scrape together. The milk was warmed gently and water was added to make it go further. I sat back on the bed, across it, with pillows behind my head and shoulders to soften the impact of the protruding window-sill. My useless lower limbs were splayed out in front of me across the pink flannelette sheet. My dad and mother sat one on each side of me.

'Ready, lad?' All I could do was wag my head up and down. I didn't trust myself to speak.

And then they started. First they saturated the lint at the corners with milk and water; then they began to ease, and pull. A dabbing with the cloth, more liquid, and then more gentle tugging ...

I don't remember much about the next two hours or so because I kept going off into a dream world, and then being jerked back to reality by the removal of some shred of lint more deeply buried than the rest. I blubbered and blabbered without control or shame, but they carried on steadfastly.

'Stick it, lad. Soldier on.'

By teatime, my legs were free of their poisonous encumbrances and had been cleaned and disinfected. They began to heal from that time on. As a reward, I was treated to rugby biscuits for my tea from Tempest's, the little grocer's shop down Garnett Street. They were large sweet biscuits, oval-shaped: they were hard-iced on one side in pink, white or yellow, and over the thin icing was a layer of shredded coconut: they came three to the packet and the packets cost twopence each. My mother could ill afford this luxury after the doctor's charges but I was still her lad, and she wanted to make a fuss of me after what we had all been through that afternoon. I pitied myself then and for weeks afterwards, but now I know the ordeal must have been far, far worse for my mother and father.

Billy Bunter and Dixon Hawke, now joined by Sexton Blake, stood by me; and gradually the sun began to shine again.

When I could support my own weight once more, Dad got me a walking-stick from somewhere. It was man-sized and thus too big for me, light amber in colour and fashioned from thick bamboo, with a large knob at the top for a handle. My right leg was still very sore, though now it was under the influence of soothing ointments instead of harsh antiseptics, and the stick was a boon to me. The three of us – Dad, the stick and I – would go for walks together, short ones at first but growing carefully longer with each day. One evening we were traversing the quarter of a mile or so from our house to the Hippodrome. I found it easier to get along if I turned my right foot outwards, which seemed to take some of the strain off the seared skin on the inside of my shin.

'Give over!' my dad ordered, sharply.

'Give over what?'

'Walking with your foot stuck out like that. Keep it straight forward. No, not timber-toed, just straight out in front of you.'

'It hurts, Dad – '

'I don't give a sod. We can't have you walking like a barmpot for the rest of your life.'

To this day, despite all the parades, drilling and marching I did during five years in the Services, I still check occasionally (and especially when moving about a stage) that my feet are going out in front of me 'straight forward'.

Romance can beckon at any age, and it beckoned to me strongly while I was still in Standard Two.

On light evenings, with plenty of time in hand before the Twenty Past Eight, I would sometimes walk round to where Eva Scott lived. She was my heart-throb at school, and although never a word had passed between us, many were the lovelorn glances we had exchanged during the communal music-class that was a regular feature at Hanson Juniors. Roughly half the school would be assembled in the Main Hall to sing together songs like *Sweet and Low*, *Oh Dear, What Can The Matter Be?*, *Strawberry Fair*, *Golden Slumbers* and *My Bonnie Lies Over The Ocean*. Under the dark, crusader-cropped hair with its thick fringe kissing her curved eyebrows, Eva's chocolate-brown eyes would lock with mine in mutual devotion, and we knew without ever speaking that we were meant for each other by the gods. Then the session would end and we would have to go our separate ways, back to those diabolical preoccupations with sums and elementary English, aching secretly for the next time we would sing together or pass each other silently on errands about the school.

It was because we had never actually exchanged conversation that I decided to make these little evening excursions to Shakespeare Street, just in case there should happen a time when she would be walking along its pavement too, and we might thus break this eternal and frustrating silence, safely away from the canes and confines of Hanson Juniors.

I stood on the opposite side of the street one evening, and looked across at her house. Eva hadn't been to school for days and I was worried in case she had fallen ill. What would the world be without her, should the worst happen? Such a thing hardly bore thinking about. What I was staring at filled me with apprehension, for the door was tightly shut and there were no lights inside the house, upstairs or down. Worse still, the windows on both floors were rain-streaked and devoid of curtains. Oh dear, what could the matter be? This was a ghost of the cheerful little house I had come to know so well. The riddle had to be solved, and with my heart in my mouth I crossed over and tapped on the house next door.

'They've gone, lad. Moved to Crossflatts, I believe.' This was a world away – somewhere near a foreign township called Bingley – and I knew I was never going to see Eva Scott again. She must have been transferred to a different school. My bonnie might just as well lie over the ocean, for good.

'Thanks, missis. Goodnight.'

I walked home at a snail's pace with my head bent, and was in long before the Twenty Past Eight howled like a banshee across the evening sky. I sprawled on the green sofa, my head against its raised end, and cogitated on the misery of a future that would be totally meaningless without Eva. I ate no supper, and this naturally upset my parents. I had always gulped my Oxo down, no matter what.

'What's up wi' our Les?'

'Don't ask me ...'

I stayed withdrawn and quiet for the rest of the evening. What was the sense in speech? Who could possibly understand my predicament? Albert was out. Whom could I turn to for a speck of comfort? What could my parents know of young love blighted, of devastation, of the long and lonely life that now lay ahead of their forsaken middle son? The world was devoid of hope.

Honoré de Balzac once wrote: 'First love is a kind of vaccination which saves a man from catching the complaint a second time.' He didn't know our Les; the medicine didn't help me in the slightest.

Chapter Five

❖

The Start of the Slump

We were now at the start of the nineteen-thirties, a period that W.H. Auden once described as 'the low, dishonest decade'. Ramsay Macdonald's Labour Government was in the middle of its tenure, and its measures seemed half-hearted and ineffectual. Unemployment was steadily growing worse, and cracks were beginning to appear in the social structure. The cinema and the public reading-room became the refuge of the workless, and all over the land men stood on street-corners in forlorn groups, smoking dog-ends and going unshaven as the canker of hopelessness began to spread. The Labour Exchange became a hated institution and, although men went there regularly to collect their means of subsistence, only a few jobs were ever available, making the name itself nothing but a mockery. After unemployment benefit ran out, its recipients were reduced to 'transitional payments', and finally to the indignity of public assistance.

Because of the tenor of the times, Sands and Grant began to extend both the scope and area of their activities. New stunts began to be developed. These were ten-minute duologues and were largely self-written, though I seem to remember that some of the material we heard on the wireless was subtly incorporated. They always featured a know-all and witty professional with a dim-witted and recalcitrant assistant. *The Plumber* had my dad in faded boiler-suit and small bowler hat perched on top of a ginger wig, instructing Uncle Jack as his apprentice in the finer points of household plumbing. I still have part of the script for this, written out in my uncle's spidery hand, with many cuts and revisions incorporated.

JACK: (entering with large bucket) Hi, hi mister!
BERT: Hello! What do you want, young man?
JACK: Can you tell me where I can get two ton o' sand?
BERT: What do you want two ton o' sand for?
JACK: Me father's brought a camel home from the Middle East and we've nowhere to keep it.
BERT: You're just the lad I want. Are you looking for work?
JACK: Not if I can find summat else to do.
BERT: *Just* the lad I want, big-bodied, bull-headed and brainless! Do you know anything about plumbing?
JACK: Aye. Me father used to skin 'em in a jam factory.
BERT: (clouts him with folded newspaper) I don't mean that sort o' plums! Would you know how to wipe a joint?
JACK: Where does she live?
BERT: (clouts him again, harder) You've got me all wrong! I mean to say, do you know how to mend a gas-pipe – put a washer on a tap – bath-bottoms – owt like that?
JACK: Bath what?
BERT: Bottoms.
JACK: No ... (slow and slyly) ... but I'm willing to learn!
(Etcetera.)

The Schoolmaster had Bert Sands in threadbare mortar-board and gown, instructing Jack Grant as a backward pupil, clad in lurid blazer and microscopic cap, in the conduct of the birds and bees. And *The Parson* would make Dad turn his collar round, abandon his false teeth and gag and grimace under a low, round, black felt hat; Uncle Jack of course would be his enthusiastic but totally useless curate.

Sands and Grant.　　　　　　　　*Photo: Author's collection*

'This being Easter Sunday, we will ask Mrs Winter-
bottom to come forward and lay an egg on the altar to
celebrate.'

'This morning a special collection will be taken to
defray the expenses of a new carpet. All wishing to do
something on the carpet, please come forward and get
a piece of paper.'

They would do four or five of these stunts during an evening's
club entertainment, mixed in with single acts like Dad's cockney
monologue *Spotty* (after Bransby Williams), and his partner's
Izzy On The Phone, it being fashionable in those days to make fun
of the Jews. Each did comic songs on his own, with titles like
A-A-Atchoo! and *I Want To Go Back To My Father And Mother*,
and both would join in duets of popular chorus-numbers such as
Bye-Bye Blackbird, *Yes Sir – That's My Baby!* and *Side By Side*.

The sessions started at about seven o'clock and were restricted to Fridays, Saturdays and Sundays, when those lucky enough to be working still had money in their pockets from the Friday pay-out. Beer and stout would be consumed by all the men present. If you didn't drink good ale then, you were a cissy. And the beers in those days had colourful and resounding names like 'Bentley's Yorkshire Bitter', 'Hey's Gold Cup' and the rather splendid 'Ramsden's Stone Trough'. Shandies, port-and-lemon and a mysterious concoction called a Green Goddess were favourites with the ladies. Spirits were rarely seen on the little round tables with their wrought-iron legs, for their cost was prohibitive. Shirt-sleeved waiters used to rush about throughout the evening with laden trays of ale, delectable pork pies and packets of potato-crisps (always Smith's and always unseasoned, with a small helping of salt in a screw of blue paper at the bottom). They joined in with the songs lustily whenever they knew them, shouted orders across the long bar and yelled coarse responses to complaining customers, heedless of whether the night's artists were performing at the time or not. There would often be a raffle, which sometimes led to loud and vividly expressed differences of opinion when the results were announced by the Chairman. Half-way through the proceedings, club notices and announcements would be read out, amidst much barracking, by the pompous Concert Secretary.

The atmosphere would be thick with smoke from pipes and Woodbines, and many of the customers would be more than merry by the time the concert was over. Dad and Uncle Jack always finished up with a moralistic rhyme followed by a 'straight' and sentimental song, *Pal Of My Wandering Days*, which expressed their lifelong and undying friendship.

> *...Over the highway, over the byway,*
> *Wherever you go will always be my way;*
> *Any old weather, laughing together –*
> *PAL OF MY WAND'RING DAYS!*

Then Sands and Grant would shake hands up on the little platform, smiling fondly and trustingly at each other. That never failed to bring the house down.

Because of their increasing status as a double act, the ever-progressive Jack Grant acquired a motorcycle and side-car, and these were used to take them out and about beyond Bradford on their 'singing jobs'. The machine was very old, very large and very noisy, and the whole of our street knew when it was arriving to pick Dad up or to return him at the end of an engagement. The windows of the side-car in which he travelled, his knees bunched up beneath his chin, were made of cheap celluloid and were torn and gaping. Jack, in the saddle and resplendent in peaked cap, greatcoat, goggles and gauntlets, gave not a rap how gimcrack the whole affair looked. 'It starts – it goes – it gets us there. That's all we care about.' And so they splurged off regularly together, through the smoky environs of Bradford, hellbent for one of their various venues. The old boneshaker took them on longer and longer trips, as their reputation steadily widened. Leeds, Huddersfield, Wakefield and Halifax became frequent ports of call; soon they would spread their wings even further, up to Darlington, west into Lancashire and, in the fullness of time, as far as Blackpool and its Philharmonic Club.

One windy night they were returning from a convivial evening in Skipton with Dad crammed into his draughty cabin as usual, guarding their cases of costumes, props and sheet music. Both had imbibed, and the motor-bike's progress was somewhat uncertain. A Yorkshire bobby waved them down on a lonely country road.

'Just watch it, you two – you're all over the bloody shop wi' that thing!'

'Sorry, officer!' Jack beamed at him. 'She's seen better days, you know. Needs a good service – like me.'

The constable sniffed at them suspiciously, but there was no such thing as a breathalyser test then. 'If I had a witness,' he admonished them, 'I could have you two tonight.'

'But you haven't,' Jack pointed out, acting sober and pretending to be affronted.

'Lucky for some,' the policeman observed. Jack revved the ancient engine and prepared to make a getaway, but the stolid arm of the law had not finished with them yet.

'Hang on.' He trudged round the front of the machine and concentrated on my father now. 'What you got in them cases?'

Dad had the devil in him. He pushed open the small, decaying door, and looked carefully up and down the road before beckoning the policeman close. They were nose to nose. 'Swag,' he whispered, 'Only *swag*. Don't tell anybody.'

'Come on out o' there!' the policeman snarled. 'Now then – open up them bags.'

'Got a search-warrant?'

'Never mind about search-warrants – get 'em undone!'

'If you haven't got a search-warrant ... ' Dad hated orders of any kind. ' ... you can't boss me about. If you want these bags opened, you can open 'em yourself.' And he placed the cases directly in front of the size eleven boots.

This did not deter the constable, who knelt to snap open the catches and lift the lid of one attaché-case. As he did so a sudden blast of wind came out of nowhere, and sent song-sheets and odd pages of script fluttering all over the ditch and into the nearby hedgerows. All of a splutter, the copper staggered back to his feet. 'It's nowt but bloody music and suchlike!' he declared.

'I know,' said my father. 'And now you can pick the whole lot up again.'

And he had to.

Sadly, the engagements did not happen every week-end; that would not be our happy circumstance for years to come. And week-ends without a 'singing job' could result in a pretty thin time all round and, more often than not, a trip round to Grandma Sands's to borrow whatever Dad and I could squeeze out of her to see the family through.

Although I went to watch them work whenever my dad was appearing locally and I could talk him into taking me, Albert always fought shy of pubs and clubs; he still does, as a matter of fact. I think this was because, being older, he could see what this kind of life was doing to his father, and feared the eventual and inevitable outcome of the boozing. Dad got to like beer more and more, and sometimes the majority of his fee would be spent on what he termed 'liquid nourishment'. This often led to tremendous quarrels between him and my mother, who had to keep five mouths fed and five bodies clothed, no matter what.

The routine was always the same when he came home drunk. First, hoping vainly that he could bluff his way through, he would creep up the passage, whistle the familiar Bert Sands whistle that was known by all the family, and knock politely on his own front door. This would then be opened gently, and his silver-grey felt hat would be tossed carefully into the living-room. If Mother had not yet reached the peak of her rage, the hat would lie undisturbed and the door would then be fully opened by one of us to allow him admittance. Dad would come in, and his face would be one big grin. We could always gauge how much he had imbibed by his complexion: the more ale he had inside him, the whiter his face got; but the grin was always there, and the grey eyes always danced with unquenchable merriment. First he would make us laugh, by telling us some oddity that had happened that evening or passing on some new joke he had heard. These were sometimes vulgar but never failed to be very funny. The trouble was, if the experience or anecdote got a laugh, he would repeat it two or three times to make sure we had got the point; and this repetition often went on to the point of suffocating boredom. After that he would wolf his supper, telling us the same thing for a fourth or fifth time before Albert and I were despatched upstairs, Bill having been tucked up safely out of harm's way hours before.

Once aloft, we would listen as the fratching began, when the time came for Dad to 'poppy up' out of the evening's earnings. Albert would lie tense beside me in the darkness, saying nothing, and I would fall to wondering if all married life had to be like that: jokes and laughter, followed by personal abuse and the tearing of one another's nerves and dignity to shreds.

'You don't do right by us – I wish I'd never married you!'

'Aw, shut up, Alice. You get more like your mother every day.'

'Don't you talk to me about mothers – not with the one you've got!'

'Will you put a flaming sock in it? Nag, nag, nag, you never stop!' The shouting would go on for an hour or more before they came to bed, and frequently gave rise to loud bangs on the party-walls from disturbed neighbours.

Sometimes, when it was strictly necessary, Dad would watch points and bring back most of his 'divvy'. But even this had its drawbacks. If he had not consumed enough ale to satisfy his current requirement he would be scratchy and dissatisfied, and the domestic row could grow just as well out of his gnawing frustration. If this happened, Albert and I would quietly sing a home-composed reprimand, to the haunting tune of *The Keel Row* :

> *Father's got the mule on,*
> *The mule on, the mule on,*
> *Father's got the mule on,*
> *He hasn't had enough!*

Now the two of us used every means we could to raise money to help out. Bill was too young to weigh in, as yet. I had none of Albert's skill with his hands and was even warned off doing, or attempting to do, any small repair jobs for myself.

'Les, if that fairy-bike of yours goes wrong, leave it alone till I have time to look at it. You start messing about, you'll only make things worse.'

This was not condescension, it was a fact of life. Where Albert could simply look at a piece of wood, metal or wire and it would turn itself miraculously into a useful and lasting artifact, I was always cursed with the inability to plane any piece of timber completely flat, to paint any surface that would not end up a sticky, uneven mess, and to drive home any screw that would not do incalculable damage to its surroundings. As a result, my efforts to ameliorate the shortage of resources had to be confined to simpler and more menial tasks than Albert's. I ran errands for neighbours, whenever I could. I hunted Bradford Moor for empty bottles, to reclaim at the off-licences the odd penny or twopence deposit that in those days was an obligatory charge. I went round asking for any old rags, until I had enough of these to take to the rag-and-bone merchant's to raise a copper or two. I would often be out (once freed from school) with a sack over my shoulder, begging for tatie-peelings and any other vegetable refuse I could then sell to the piggeries at the end of Pit Lane. And I toured the local newsagents, trying for a job as a delivery-boy, but they told me I was too young and the bags would be too heavy. 'Come back when you're fourteen, son. Thicken out a bit. We won't forget you ...'

Albert of course was never short of ideas, and was forever perfecting them and putting them into practice. He made decorative wall-plaques from ornamental brass plates he had borrowed, creating plaster-of-paris castings of them which he then painted and sold. He discovered a formula for making hair-cream which consisted mainly of gum tragacanth and a few drops of *Parma Violets* purloined from my mother, and we would have done well out of this venture but could never track down enough bottles of the right shape and size for its distribution. Somehow he acquired a collection of old gramophone records, and he and Dad would place these one by one in the oven until they became soft and malleable, whereupon they were coaxed by hand into attractive black bowls with curly edges. They were then daubed in bright colours and sold off cheaply to people who could afford a few bulbs or indoor plants. 'Got their own drainage, you see,' my father would explain in his sales-talk, 'that little hole in the middle that goes on the gramophone.'

My brother scored a major triumph when he wrote away to the Great Universal Stores of Manchester and became their local representative, talking neighbours into placing mail-orders for clothes and household articles and thereby picking up a useful amount of commission. They sent him a satchel made of real leather to hold their giant catalogue. This was eventually passed on to me when Albert finished with the job, and became my school-bag, the only one I ever had.

Holidays had vanished completely from our lives now, and we had few amusements except those we could conjure up for ourselves. I was becoming an avid reader by this time, concentrating mainly on boys' magazines like *Adventure*, *Rover*, *Wizard*, *Skipper* and *The Boys' Own Paper*. Albert, noticing the fascination that reading held for me, got me to join my first public library. The nearest one to have a children's section was in Undercliffe Street, one of the steepest hills in Bradford; but the regular climb there was a small price to pay for the riches I found upon its shelves. It cost only one penny to become a member, the best pennyworth I have ever had. My library-ticket was my passport to another world and by far the best friend I possessed, outside of my family.

In 1926 Albert had stood on the street-corner with a group of lads, and they had suffered a strange visitation. A complete stranger not much older than Albert himself, well-dressed and properly-spoken, had stopped and talked to them about religion and, in particular, about the Wesleyan Methodist beliefs. The stranger was of this persuasion himself, and was going round the poorer quarters of Bradford trying to talk some of the street-corner youths into their first experience of Sunday School. His name was Kenneth Hockney, and he had a son who was destined to grow up into a world-famous painter. His name was David Hockney.

Mr Hockney's headquarters were at Eastbrook Hall, a Gothic-style building down at the bottom of Leeds Road, that was the Methodist citadel in Bradford. Largely, his cajolements fell on deaf ears that night, for most of his audience were more concerned with public bars and billiard-halls, and religion played no part in their tough and uncompromising young lives. Bravely he ploughed on with his personal crusade. And that evening he had one interested listener in my brother.

The upshot of it was that Albert went down to Eastbrook and became a Methodist. He went regularly to its classes and fellowships and found there a new friendship and understanding among people who, like himself, were trying to widen their horizons and learn more about life and its meaning than could be gleaned from pubs and clubs. He made new acquaintances, he debated on important themes, he worshipped God in the Methodist way ... and he joined the dramatic society.

Because Albert went to Eastbrook Hall, I had to go to Eastbrook Hall too, though at first only to Sunday School. Here I learned about mysterious things like Christmas Services and Harvest Festivals. And here I sang hymns that had been written from the heart.

In the upstairs schoolroom at Eastbrook, concerts would be given frequently. These were mainly of a musical or choral nature and the standard of execution was often more enthusiastic than accomplished, but they provided a very pleasant way to spend an evening. One concert turned out to be different from the rest. Albert told me he was going to be in a play, and this impressed me greatly. Light entertainment I knew something about, for after all I had watched my dad and others doing their stuff and had even, on occasion, got up on the platform and done a turn myself; and hadn't we all given of our best at Grandma's soirées? But a real play was a very ambitious project indeed. It needed confidence, a good memory, hard work and a touch of something called 'acting ability'. I was amazed at Albert's fecklessness.

Of course he got me a ticket, and of course I went. I sat and marvelled at the proper wooden stage that had been erected at one end of the schoolroom, complete with real curtains and a lighting system. And the play enthralled me. It was a highly moralistic and propagandist tract about the abolition of slavery, and my brother played the part of a negro bondsman. All the flesh on him that could be seen was covered in ebony, and the features I knew so well were quite unrecognisable under their coating of burnt cork, especially when topped off by a jet-black and very frizzy wig. He rolled his eyes magnificently, and to me played his part to perfection.

Eastbrook Hall. *Photo: Bradford Telegraph & Argus*

I decided I must play a straight part, and soon. But how would I ever get into a proper play, at my age and with absolutely no experience of straight acting? There were no junior dramatics at Eastbrook, and anyway I was hampered by my lisp and my broad Yorkshire accent. Both of these would have to go somehow, before I could be any good on the stage. So I began to listen more carefully to how the teachers spoke, and tried to emulate their diction and inflections, sounding all my aitches (many of them in the wrong place) and filling in the consonantal gaps so often encountered in the Bradford patois: 'boo-a' became 'butter', as it properly should be. I tried to avoid slang words and anything smacking of the slums in my speech. I began to think about English as a friend rather than a scholastic imposition. And I started to conquer that damned lisp, by holding my tongue further back in my mouth and sounding my sibilants through my lower front teeth. Gradually, I think I began to speak a little better.

But the opportunity to be in a real play did not present itself; so I wrote my own.

I was by this time in Miss Dickinson's class. She was a fine teacher, a strict disciplinarian and a sterling Englishwoman. She loved her native language and was never happier than when taking her forty or so charges through a new poem or introducing them to a fresh and exciting story, which she would first get us to read and then analyse for our benefit, finally throwing the subject open to question and discussion. Miss Dickinson it was who told us the story of Damon and Pythias, the famous friends of Greek legend, one of whom gave the surrender of his life as a guarantee of his comrade's return from adventures abroad. He was on the very brink of execution when the other came back, thus proving his worthiness of trust and the value of true and undying friendship. The fable intrigued me, and in one of my notebooks at home I wrote the play of *Damon and Pythias*. With some misgivings, I offered this up for the authoritative consideration of my schoolmistress. Miss Dickinson turned up trumps and actually produced the play in the classroom, in the open space in front of the long blackboard. More than that, she gave me to my delight the part of the 'heavy', the wicked king Dionysius. I revelled in it, and have loved character parts ever since. I was nine years old, and played a man of forty.

I told Lorna Phillips all about my triumph. Lorna was a year behind me at school, and had therefore not been able to see my performance; but she had to be informed of every detail, because she was my current sweetheart. The younger daughter of a local baker and confectioner, Lorna was a slim, eight-year-old china doll of a girl with long blonde hair and eyes of an incredible blueness. We had exchanged very respectful notes through the railings that divided the boys' playground from the girls', and this had led to hurried meetings out in Byron Street after school had finished for the day. Lorna's older sister Gwen encouraged this little idyll, and it wasn't long before I was going over to their street in the evenings to play rounders with them, on the cobbles outside Mr Phillips's aromatic shop. The shop window was always filled with rows of new, crusty loaves and tiers of scrumptious-looking cream-cakes. I had my first cake filled with fresh dairy cream at Lorna's birthday party when she was nine, and was introduced to everyone by the worldly-wise Gwen as 'our Lorna's young man', much to the hilarity of the grown-ups present and my own acute discomfiture. The evening was a great success, and I presented Lorna with three tiny handkerchiefs that my mother had somehow managed to provide.

This particular childhood dalliance ended somewhat abruptly one evening, when I had gone up there to play our usual rounders. Gwen, longer in the leg than either of us, taller, quicker and suppler, was an expert at the game and rapidly piled up her score. I limped behind, a bad second, striving to keep up some semblance of male superiority, and failing miserably. Lorna had hardly scored at all. She was bad at hitting the ball and even worse at reaching the various bases before being run out, the ball hitting the marker accurately, thrown usually by the mercurial Gwen before Lorna could get anywhere near it in her headlong flight. There were other children present and playing, but I had no eyes for them. At one point I was flinging myself round the pitch at a tremendous rate, trying to impress and also build up my score, when the heel of my old shoe suddenly flew off and scudded away down the street. I stood there, embarrassed in front of the Phillips sisters and their friends, not knowing quite what to do in this calamity. Completely mistress of the situation, Gwen retrieved the offending article and brought it back to me.

'Your heel's come off.'

'I know.' My voice sounded strangled.

'Better go home and change your shoes, then.'

'I can't.'

'Why not?' Gwen was keen to know.

'Just can't, that's all.'

She looked down at the battered heel and then at the remainder of my shoe. Then she looked at the other shoe. My footwear had been well polished by my assiduous mother, but there was no disguising the ravages of age and hard wear.

'Those aren't your best shoes, are they?'

'They're all I've got.'

Lorna and her friends had gathered round us now in an attentive knot. They were all of them better dressed than I, and their shoes were sturdy and well-made. I could see that because I was staring down at the ground, not wishing to meet anyone's eyes.

'You're not rich, then?' Gwen's tone had turned cool and distant.

'We're all right.'

She handed me back the damning evidence of my social inadequacy, and I rammed it in my pocket. Perhaps Grandad Sands, a cobbler of no mean repute by now, would be able to fix the heel back on for me; I knew I should never be able to do this for myself. But Gwen hadn't finished yet.

'You're not good enough for our Lorna, you aren't.'

The youthful assembly waited for me to re-establish myself somehow, but it was beyond me.

'Goodnight.' I turned my back on all of them, and went home.

It was quite impossible for well-placed tradespeople like the Phillipses to realise just how Grant Street and Garnett Street were situated. Clothes were the last in our long list of priorities. We had a bare minimum of wardrobe, and renewals (when vitally necessary) were worrisome and costly. At this time, apart from old trousers, shirts and pullovers, my father had only one good suit, and this was kept for very special occasions indeed. He had a presentable raincoat, two caps and a felt hat. Nestling in the large cupboard in his bedroom was his most prized possession, a dinner-jacket and black trousers donated to him by Uncle Jack, but these were for professional use only. My mother had one decent dress, a good coat for going out in, various threadbare skirts and cardigans, and three pinafores (one on, one off and one in the wash). Albert and I had jackets and pants but these rarely matched, and were almost without exception second-hand. We had no cupboard in our bedroom, and our entire wardrobe still hung on hooks behind the bedroom door in rough, brown-paper covers.

We patronised the second-hand shops when we could, and what new clothes or shoes we did get normally came by way of a 'club cheque'. Various organisations existed in town, (usually incorporating the word 'provident' in their business headings) by whom, if your references were good and your past payment-record impeccable, you could be issued with a credit note. These came in varying amounts according to your circumstances, and could be exchanged for goods at clothiers' and outfitters' shops. Repayment was made to the 'provident' financiers by weekly instalments, and the whole transaction always included a hefty rake-off for them. So a pair of shoes that had a retail price of, say, four shillings and elevenpence could cost you up to six shillings or so when you took the commission into account, which the poor and sorely-pressed customers seldom did.

No Gwen, we weren't rich, not in the way you understood the word; but in our own way, we had riches beyond compare. We had deep love for one another, we had our self-respect and, above all, we had the good sense to laugh in the face of adversity. My father said one day:

'When I can't afford Woodbines any more, I'll smoke Three Nuns – none yesterday, none today and none tomorrow.'

1931 was Albert's final year at Hanson, when he was to sit the examination for his school and matriculation certificates. I had no doubt at all that he would pass both with ease, but there were forces at work that I had not reckoned with.

He was sixteen years of age now, and the grown man was stirring strongly within him. During the early months of the year he had become infatuated with a neighbour's daughter, an attractive and nubile young lady, his senior by some six or seven years. We all go through this 'older woman' syndrome with results that are usually disastrous in varying degrees; and although I did not know it then, my turn would come, eventually.

Albert was hauled over the coals by his mother and father alike, but this made no difference to his adulation. He went out for walks with Hilda, he took her to the pictures and on one occasion to the Palace Theatre, a variety house down in town. They seemed to be inseparable. Mother went after them like an avenging fury and insulted the girl openly, accusing her of 'stealing her lad' in front of all the theatre-leaving crowds in Manchester Road. 'She's *common*,' said the girl, and walked away from the disturbance. Albert followed her.

My father, furious at this, took Albert to task in the little living-room at Grant Street, when he got home.

'You'll give over seeing that young woman!'

'I won't, Dad.'

'Upsetting your mother like that – she's heartbroken. I'll give that lass "common". Now listen to me! You'll knock it off or else I'll – I'll –'

'You'll what?' I had never seen my brother so frozen and so still. I looked at them both, stunned. I could make no sense of this awful crisis and conflicting loyalties were splitting me in half.

'I'll belt the living daylights out of you!' my father threatened.

Albert was trembling slightly, but whether with fear, embarrassment or determination I had no means of knowing. He was taller than my dad but slighter in build, and certainly no match for the stocky, broad-shouldered bull of a man he now confronted.

93

'I'll live my own life, Dad. And I'll pick my own friends.'

'You'll do as I say!'

And then my father hit him, the flat of his hand landing with tremendous impact on his son's left cheek. Albert swayed heavily but he kept his balance, both mentally and physically. Then, very slowly, he turned his head and pointed to the other cheek.

'Belt that one now, Dad.'

Eastbrook Hall's teachings had cut quite deep.

Ex-Sergeant Sands saw some of his own wartime courage and tenacity staring him in the face. It proved too much for him, and he broke down and cried like a child. My brother never shed a single tear.

There were succeeding quarrels just as bitter as this one, but it would do no good to detail them here. Parents consulted parents, and still the unfortunate liaison went on unabated. Then one day it came to an abrupt halt. I never knew what brought this about and I have never discussed it with Albert; but I have little doubt that he made up his own mind that things had gone far enough. Suddenly he wasn't seeing the girl any more, and this was entirely of his own volition. After a week or two her father came along the street and up the passage, to have it out with us. The old man hobbled badly, because he had had a stroke.

'You've got to let them get together again. You ought to see our Hilda – that lass is pining herself away.'

'Let her pine,' my mother snapped. And that was the end of the matter.

In the summer, Albert sat for his matriculation. The examining body failed to recognise his capabilities, and he left Hanson School without either of the certificates he had worked so long and so hard to win.

At first, like so many others, he could not find a job however hard he tried. Autumn came, and with it the early snows. Father and son now often sat in silence in the evenings sharing a common need, each taking his turn to study the Situations

Vacant column in the *Telegraph and Argus*. Albert would write off letters of application when he could afford the stamps, but Dad had almost given up this seemingly pointless quest after three solid years of unemployment. Then Albert would go off down to Eastbrook Hall, which brought us both a good deal of solace during those dejected days. As often as I could I would go there with him, but he of course was part of an older element and few of my young Sunday School chums were there on the weekday evenings. So I would tag along behind my brother, always at a respectful distance. This must often have driven him to distraction, but he rarely gave any sign of impatience or intolerance; indeed, he made a joke of it.

Only once did he give any sort of hint that this spaniel-like devotion was perhaps becoming something of a trial in these days of his early manhood. He had been to a Wesley Guild meeting one Tuesday, and I had passed the time down in the junior schoolroom, picking out a popular tune of the day on the piano-keys with my stubby forefinger.

> *Happy days are here again,*
> *The skies above are clear again,*
> *Let us sing a song of cheer again –*
> *Happy days are here again!*

At length I heard voices in the corridor, coming from the open door of the little room where the group-discussion had taken place; I was out there in a flash, in search of my big brother.

Albert was walking away up the corridor with a small band of friends, male and female. They were laughing and talking together. Someone drew his attention to my hovering presence and he stopped, looked back, and laughed.

'There he is, then. Have you seen my little lap-dog?'

This was an Albert I did not know. This was a separate person, growing into an adult, who had no urgent need of the fawning attentions of a kid brother, especially when he was flexing his intellectual muscles among people of his own age and kind. I backed down the corridor, making to return to the junior schoolroom and its more friendly associations.

A girl detached herself from the group and walked back towards me. She seemed older than Albert, and had a mass of light auburn hair and the kindest eyes I have ever seen. She comforted me, took my hand, and walked me back to join their company.

'He's all right, Doris. A little thing like that doesn't bother our Les.' Albert believed this to be true; he would have bitten out his tongue rather than hurt me.

Her name, I later learned, was Doris Langley. Albert had no particular attachment to her at that time; but a few short years later he was to marry her, and they would enjoy a long, productive and enviably happy life together.

My late sister-in-law was the nearest approach to an angel on earth that I have ever met.

Unlike many other school-leavers who, old men before their time, simply became drifters and joined up with their elders in the reading-room, at the Labour Exchange or on the street-corner, Albert kept looking until he found a job with some kind of future in it. He was finally accepted as an apprentice by the engineering firm of John Hardaker and Sons in Bowling Back Lane, who specialised in the design and manufacture of jacquard looms. Though catering for its needs, he had avoided going 'into t'mill'. No mill for Albert; and no mill for me, if I could help it. His apprenticeship was to last from the age of sixteen to that of twenty-one, and his starting-pay was five shillings a week. He left home at half-past seven in the morning and returned at five minutes to six in the evening, as regular as clockwork. We would see him briefly as he downed a hot meal and then he would wash and change and be off again, perhaps in search of second-hand tools or textbooks or, two or three times a week now, away to his beloved Eastbrook Hall. Our relationship was as strong as ever, but his spare-time company was now rarely available to me. So I became something of a loner for a year or two, for at this stage I did not make friends easily. I had my books and was perfectly content with my own company. And there was always the cinema, when you could afford it. Little did I know it, but a new and compelling world was about to open up for me.

Bradford had two main theatres at that time, and both were flourishing. The Alhambra was its pride and joy, offering touring shows on the grand scale interspersed with weeks of first class variety bills. I could rarely afford the price of admission, even to the 'gods'; but if you stood very near the big scenery-doors in Morley Street at the rear of the theatre, you could hear a smattering of what was going on inside. I was there most Saturday nights; and most Saturday nights, it was raining.

Not very far away was the Prince's Theatre, a white-fronted building that housed something called a repertory company. Here the seats were much cheaper, and here I saw my first professional production of a straight play. It was a Saturday matinée, and it cost me threepence to go in by a side-entrance and clamber up the endless stone steps to the gallery. The play was Bram Stoker's *Dracula*, and the actors seemed like deities to me. I came away in a daze of happiness and excitement, vowing I would go again as soon as I could save up the money; and next time I would try and afford a programme, so that I could personally identify these supernatural beings with their strong and colourful personalities, their immaculate delivery of lines, their total self-confidence and their evident devotion to their world of make-believe. Yes, I would go again. And again. And again. The Theatre was beginning to take its grip.

Chapter Six

---- ❖ ----

The Heart of the Slump

'Here's a threepenny bit, Les. Nip round the corner to Fred Prince's and get your hair cut. You're on the platform Friday night ...'

Sands and Grant were never happier than when they were 'on the platform'. But paid bookings sometimes became scarce for, as with all performers, a club comic's life is no bed of roses. When this regular blight occurred, they would make their own opportunities to give a show, often 'free, gratis and for nothing' as Dad liked to put it. This kept their hand in, and brought pleasure to a lot of people who badly needed and could not afford to pay for such diversion.

A small concert party was formed, and with this they toured hospitals, old folks' homes and institutions for the poor and needy of all kinds. They were the star turn of course, doing their singles and doubles to provide most of a full evening's entertainment, but they had sturdy and enthusiastic support. There was a lady soprano, who gave lusty renditions of such popular classics as *Song of Songs*, *My Heart is Like a Singing Bird* and *The Flight of Ages*; she was a charming and motherly lady with an Eton crop, whose name I have clean forgotten but whose sweeping ball-dress I shall always remember, as it seemed to be composed entirely of multi-coloured glass beads. My cousin Mildred (Uncle Jack's daughter) was training to be a dancer, and would be there with her partner Gwendolyn to trip the gavotte and other light fantastics. The accompanist was plump Arnold Pearson, one of the town's outstanding pianists, who was eminent enough to be resident at the Textile Hall, the largest and most grandiose of Bradford's clubs. I made up the group as 'juvenile lead', complete with my very own dinner-jacket suit and black patent-leather pumps. I did Stanley Holloway monologues, and sang songs that were mainly comic ditties my father had discarded or rousing chorus-songs of the time, such as Jack Hulbert's *My Hat's on the Side of my Head* and Jessie Matthews's evergreen *Over my Shoulder*. We were a happy and united troupe who served to lighten, I think, many a dark evening for the poor unfortunates in those drab little chambers, wards and assembly halls.

All this ceased abruptly when Dad and Uncle Jack fell out. They could be a scratchy pair, especially after they had downed a few pints; and somehow they always managed to find some bevvy, wherever they were playing.

Dad came home one night from a professional engagement at Brownroyd Labour Club, with a face like a wet Monday morning.

'It's Jack,' he told my mother. 'We've finished, lass. Finished.'

'What over?' Mother saw even grimmer days ahead, if the club-singing should peter out.

'Nay, it were summat and nowt, really. But he ended up telling me I'm no bloody good because I'm out o' work.'

Mum was incensed. 'Who does he think he is?'

'Know what he said? I was there in the dressing-room, brushing me dinner-jacket off, and he said "If it wasn't for me, you wouldn't have the clothes you're stood up in."'

'He *never*! What are you going to do, Albert?'

'Send that bloody suit straight back.'

Next day when I came home for my dinner, there was a large brown-paper parcel in the centre of the table, neatly addressed in Dad's copperplate handwriting to 'Mr Jack Hemmans, 111 Curzon Road, Bradford Moor.' He had seen fit to deny Uncle Jack the professional courtesy of using his stage-name; Jack Hemmans he had been christened and Jack Hemmans he would be called, especially for an event so solemn and personal as this.

The Concert Party.   *Photo: Author's collection*

'Les, take that up to one-one-one on your way back to school.'

'It isn't on me way, Dad,' I said, trying to evade an uncomfortable responsibility. 'It's out of me way.'

'You'll take it anyroad.'

My dinner had lost its savour. Soon I was walking slowly up yet another hill, towards Curzon Road. In addition to the cachet of a regular income, Uncle Jack and Aunt Gertie had one other advantage over us. They lived in a 'through house', which meant they had a brightly-painted front door in the road itself and a less impressive brown door at the rear, giving on to their microscopic yard and thence to the back-snicket that ran parallel with the row of houses.

I went as usual to the back. I still half-believe that garish front door was only for show, because I never saw anyone enter or leave 'one-one-one' by it. Throbbing with embarrassment, I knocked on the brown-painted door. She took her time, but it was finally opened by Aunt Gertie. Normally she was a charming and gracious lady, if somewhat over-conscious

101

of her social superiority; on this occasion she had a face of carved stone.

'Hello, Leslie.'

'Me dad's sent this.'

'Yes, we were expecting it. Er – how's your mother?'

'She's all right.' Then, this being Aunt Gertie at her snootiest, I was careful to add: 'Thank you.'

'Thank *you*, Leslie.'

She took the parcel without further ado and shut the door in my face. Unlike all the rest of the family, Aunt Gertie never called me 'Les'.

Dad carried on with his solo work as best he could, but with the impulsive cessation of Sands and Grant as a club attraction and his valiant struggle to re-establish himself as a single act, money got even scarcer at 11 Grant Street. The next few months were a time of domestic strain and severe deprivation.

Now and then we were invited into their homes by other relations who were doing rather better than we were, and given a slap-up meal to tide us over. We could always rely on this at Cousin Nellie's in Dudley Hill, some three or four miles from our own home. Nellie Widdop was my mother's cousin and took care of her widowed father in a little back-to-back house with an enormous yard that always looked as though it had been newly sandpapered. We would walk to Cousin Nellie's on a Sunday morning, hoping the weather would keep up until we got there, Mother and I taking turns to propel my three-year-old brother Bill in his push-chair. Once at the house, the pinafored Nellie and her apple-cheeked father, Uncle Willie, would ply us with hot food and cups of tea until our unaccustomed stomachs were at bursting-point. Whereupon, he would retire to his armchair with *Reynold's News* and be incommunicado for the rest of the afternoon, while he solved England's problems by the mental creation of a Socialist utopia. Mother and Cousin Nellie would meanwhile immerse themselves in huge piles of family photographs that recalled scenes of happy holidays, family gatherings and the good old days before the Slump. And I myself would browse, burping gently, through the magazines that always lay in a welcoming pile on the little bamboo whatnot ... *Everybody's*, *Illustrated*, *Woman's Weekly*, and *The Happy Mag.* among them. It was a great age for popular magazines and I have been devoted to them ever since. At five o'clock we would be treated to a massive high tea and then, after a necessary respite to let the food settle, we would launch on the long trek home. This was usually as dusk was falling.

We were returning thus one autumn evening, with mists beginning to gather and the gas-lamps along Bowling Back Lane doing their best to light our way, when my mother's keen eyes spotted something lying on the pavement just ahead of us.

'Here you are, lad, hang on to our Bill while I have a look.' She gave me the handle of Bill's push-chair and advanced cautiously on the mysterious object. 'Hey, Les – it's a wallet or summat!'

And indeed it was. Made of leather, it was old, tattered and positively bulging. My mother's brown eyes shone. 'I'm having that!' We looked round us, but there was nobody else on the street and no curtains were twitching – so she picked it up and hid it under her green shawl, a form of dress she then favoured which harked back to her mill-lass days.

'Aren't you going to have a look inside?'

'Whisht!' For some reason she was hissing now. 'Wait till we get to t'next lamp.'

We hurried on guiltily, and stopped under the flickering yellow gas-light. Her hand shaking with excitement, my mother flicked the little rusty catch on the wallet, and opened it wide to see what wealth had come our way so unexpectedly. Then she gave a dry retch, and flung it as far away from her as possible. The wallet was full of human dung.

As she tried to clean her hands in a nearby puddle, we heard boys cackling hoarsely from some close hiding-place.

'Bloody fenians – I'll murder 'em!' Straightening, Mum looked all about her in a fury, trying to track them down. But there was nothing and nobody to be seen, and all we could hear was the scrape of hobnailed boots on cobbles as the rapscallions made their escape into the night ...

There was real poverty in Bradford now; but many people were worse off than we were, as dad constantly reminded us. We were having bread-and-dripping for our supper one night and I was grousing because the bread was stale –

'Tastes funny.' I had seen my mother scrape green mould off the loaf, and wasn't fancying my share anyway.

'What's wrong with it?' My father jabbed at the offending slice with his knife.

'Tastes funny – and it's hard, an' all.'

The grey eyes looked at me with more than a hint of Grandma Sands's gravity in them.

'It's harder where there's none.'

In many families, indeed there was none; and some, despite the infrequent charity hand-outs, were on the point of starvation. The authorities met their plight with a stony indifference. There was no National Assistance then, and nothing like Supplementary Benefit; there was only the Means Test, and after that a grim struggle for survival. My mother told us of a war-widow and her small family in Peel Street, whose few possessions were distrained for non-payment of rates. The Council eventually came and took all their furniture away for sale at auction to defray the debt, and all they had left were the beds they slept in, that being apparently a proviso under the Poor Law. Their gas had been cut off, and they were existing in the downstairs room of their terraced slum-house, sitting on orange-boxes round an upturned barrel, on which stood the paraffin-lamp that was their only means of heating and illumination. Later on, in high school, I would learn and remember all my life the self-obituary delivered by Sir Robert Peel in the last century, when he succeeded in his battle to repeal the Corn Laws: 'I shall leave a name sometimes remembered with good will in the abodes of those who labour and earn their daily bread by the sweat of their brow, when they shall recruit their exhausted strength with abundant and untaxed food, the sweeter because it is not leavened by a sense of injustice.' I wonder if Sir Robert ever looked down from some politician's paradise and witnessed some of the injustices that

A tram in Leeds Road passing Eastbrook Hall c.1920.

Photo: Christopher Pratt

subsequently took place in that street that bore his name? And loads of other mean streets, up and down Britain …

I will mention only one further enduring image typical of the Hungry Thirties. I was coming home from Grandma Sands's one afternoon, alone – Dad having stopped off at the Red House to buy himself a gill out of the florin or so we had been able to extract from her – when I saw a woman walking by herself down the centre of Garnett Street. She was tall and had been well-proportioned but her cheeks were hollow now, and her shoulders gaunt and bony under the thin shawl she had slung round her neck. The shawl was stone-coloured, and her nearly ankle-length skirt was shapeless and of brown fustian. Long, dark auburn hair streamed gloriously down her back over the threadbare shawl, and on her left arm she held a brown paper carrier-bag by only one of its string handles, so that the rest of it swung slackly open.

She was singing some old Irish song, and her voice was loud and striking; deep for a woman's, but true and clear in every note. I followed her down the street, not feeling sorry for her (beggars had become commonplace in the Slump) but interested to know what she was about, and wondering if perhaps she were beginning to lose her mind. And then I realised what she was up to, because down the dreaded Garnett Street doors began to open; and people, mostly women, came out to drop little offerings into the carrier-bag. There were a few pennies and ha'pennies among the gifts, but mainly they consisted of scraps of food and cheap, disposable, household items that the vagrant might be able to sell for sustenance. I saw odd clothes-pegs go into the bag, a quarter-packet of tea, a string of safety pins, a couple of men's ties and a card of pearl buttons. I listened to the song, so beautifully sung, and wished I could do something to help. But I had nothing at all to give to the lady. So halfway down Garnett Street, I turned round and went home … as the voice faded gradually away in the distance, strong, true, proud and undefeated.

That was my Bradford, in 1931.

Our staple diet was fish and chips; and there are some who still say that what steered this country safely through the Slump was not the ship of State, but the humble fish-and-chip shop. A fairish piece of cod, battered and fried in beef dripping, shorn of bones and pieces of skin, cost tuppence-ha'penny. Fish-cakes, which consisted of two large slices of potato sandwiching a morsel of mashed fish and the whole again fried in golden batter, were invariably delicious, and set you back only three ha'pence each. A pennorth of chips would provide a meal in itself, if you could rustle up two slices of bread-and-marge to go with it. And I deliberately made myself a favourite at the local chip-shops, as we called them, so that in addition to my family order I would be handed a bag of 'scraps' – spare pieces of batter and chips that were scraped from the corners and sides of the holding-bays to keep these clean and uncluttered. I would sprinkle these delicious morsels over the plates when we sat down to the meal, as a tasty garnish; and I always made sure I got the lion's share. Hutton's on Barkerend Road was the best chip-shop in our area, because Mr Hutton's fish-cakes were outsize, and he always put pepper in them.

At the meal itself I copied Albert, and made thick sandwiches out of my allotted portion. This custom has stayed with me; and in good London restaurants I have often shamed my sensitive and discerning wife by making butties out of my lemon sole or grilled plaice, and eating these as discreetly as possible behind the cover of some large, open menu. Old habits die hard, I suppose, and the habits of the Slump die hardest of all.

Christmas luckily brought Dad a lot of bookings and, although this meant that Albert, Bill and I were largely left to our own devices during the three-day break, food for once was plentiful and there were good Christmas presents for us all. I was given a long-coveted Diana air-rifle and on Christmas Night, while dad was no doubt singing his heart out and 'pulling the place down' as he always described it, Albert and I took up stations in the yard and used up all the slugs and pellets by firing them at Inmans' red dustbin at the far end.

Whether we actually penetrated it or not I shall never know, because we did not dare go along and look; but I remember Mr Inman, an insurance agent, being more pale and withdrawn than ever for some days afterwards; however, maybe that was merely the after-effects of Christmas indulgence on the part of the penny-a-week man.

And then we were into 1932. I would soon be eleven, and this was my scholarship year. Hanson Junior School was beginning to be a great solace and refuge for me from the trials and tribulations of Grant Street in the Slump. My teacher was still Miss Dickinson. Encouraged by Albert I was working hard, and I sat in the centre of the back row slap next to the outstanding brain of the class, Miss Dora Watson. I was following Grandma's advice and trying to mix with those I considered better endowed than myself. And I was determined to win that scholarship in the summer, for not only did I desperately want to follow in Albert's footsteps and go on to secondary school, but also I had been promised by my dad any bicycle of my choice, if I got through the all-important test.

And so summer came and, in the mildest of weather, Sands and Grant resolved their differences – and I won my scholarship.

I dashed home from school with the buff envelope in my hand in which was the roneoed verification, and thrust it at my father.

'What's this say, then?'

'Have a look, Dad – go on, have a look!'

He didn't need to. The self-satisfied grin on my moon face had told him the result already.

'Right, lad.' He leaned over and ruffled my hair until it stood on end. 'Tomorrow we'll go down in town and get that bike.'

And, true to his word, we went down together to a shop called Baines's in a little narrow lane called Piccadilly which ran parallel with the important shopping thoroughfare of Darley Street. Here my dad signed a hire-purchase agreement for the bike of my dreams, a sports model with drop handle-bars and an ivory-and-black frame that rejoiced in the name of

The Talbot Dog.   *Photo: Bradford Telegraph & Argus*

a Raleigh Super Sports. It cost five pounds, nineteen shillings and sixpence, and took a long time to pay for by weekly instalments. But then, and for years afterwards, it was my pride and joy.

On one of our jaunts together to keep up the payments at Baines's we again passed the Talbot Hotel, and I reminded my father of how he had told me the fable years before that the stone dog over the entrance, whenever it heard midnight strike, would jump down off its pedestal, run round Forster Square and then jump back up again to its place of honour.

'Do you know, Dad,' I told him, now an eleven-year-old sceptic and believing myself almost a man of the world, 'I fell for that. Just because you said it, I really believed it – for years.'

He stopped in the middle of Kirkgate and looked at me very seriously.

'It's true, is that.'

'Gerron!'

'Come back here.'

We returned to the Talbot, and he gazed up at the black and lowering statue reverently.

'I bet you've never seen it yourself!' I taunted him.

'Just look at him. Go on, have a good look. Now, what's that dog made of?'

'Stone, I think.' I wasn't sure.

'Look at them ears – can you see 'em wagging?'

'Course not! He's made of stone – definitely.'

'Right, then. He's stone-*deaf*, isn't he?' Then as I nodded, beginning to comprehend, he went on poker-faced: 'But you can bank on it, if ever he *does* hear that Town Hall clock strike twelve, he'll be down off that pedestal like a bloody shot.'

That was my father. He'd been willing to wait years for the pleasure of delivering the pay-off line – and he did it to perfection.

During the summer break, my brother decided that the two of us must have a holiday. Gone was the halcyon era of weeks in Blackpool and trips to Morecambe, for our exchequer would no longer permit of any such extravagances. We must have a cheap holiday that would cost us next to nothing. Albert gave the matter his deep consideration and had many lengthy consultations with his new friend Edward Fox, whom we always referred to as 'Oscar'. And in the end the two pals came up with a solution.

In those days, hiking was the most popular of all working-class pastimes. It was dirt-cheap, it got you out in the country and it did you good physically, mentally and spiritually. In fact, a favourite song of the time was *I'm Happy When I'm Hiking*. Every week-end hordes of devotees made off for the Dales, clad in open-necked shirts and khaki shorts, with bulging rucksacks on their backs. Those of sufficient means or enterprise would carry with them a small tent, a groundsheet and provisions, and would camp out whenever the weather permitted. Albert and Oscar knew one or two lads who had their own tents, and so the equipment could be borrowed for the week when Albert would be off work for the firm's annual holiday. Arrangements were made, and they acquired not one tent but two, one for the three of us to sleep in and a smaller one to hold what groceries we could muster for the golden week.

I did not know in advance that Eastbrook Hall had organised its own camping holiday, for those who could afford to pay expenses; and the same week that we would be in the rustic splendour and fresh air of Ben Rhydding, they would be under canvas some two miles away at Burley-in-Wharfedale. The Eastbrook Hall contingent included several attractive girls and Albert and Oscar, both now seventeen, no doubt considered this not at all a bad thing to have within striking distance on a carefree holiday.

Our plans were made firm, and Albert cycled over to Ben Rhydding, found a suitable farmstead that would supply milk from the cow and clear cold water, and booked a corner in one of their fields for our exclusive use for seven days.

Of course, we could not afford any form of transport other than our bikes; and Oscar did not have one. He offered to try and scrounge one, but then Albert came up with his brilliant idea.

'We'll have a *midnight hike!*'

This took our fancy straightaway. To leave home on the stroke of twelve and go stomping off through Bradford and out towards the Dales, our rucksacks on our backs, would not only be fashionable but also tremendously exciting. Perhaps, I thought secretly, we might even see the odd stone mastiff galloping round Forster Square as we passed through.

The longed-for Saturday night came at last and there we all sat, at a late supper in Grant Street.

'Eat all you can,' my mother cautioned us. 'I don't know how you'll get on this week without me there to stuff your insides for you.' So we all ate an enormous meal and then, nearing midnight, Albert and Oscar disappeared beneath a gigantic weight of gear and I was handed a smaller rucksack and the vital groundsheets to take care of. We departed as the Town Hall was striking the witching hour, much to my mother's misgivings and my father's open glee.

'I reckon it'll be about dawn when we get there,' Albert calculated. 'Light enough to see anyway, and get these tents up. Then we can have a good kip before we get down to this holiday caper.'

I have never been much of a walker, and was feeling pretty faint by the time we had got through the centre of Bradford and were pressing on up Manningham Lane.

'You all right, Les?'

'Aye. I think so.'

'Come on, then. Best foot forward!'

My brother had always been lean and wiry, and was a great tramper and cyclist; Oscar had a seventeen-year-old's determination not to be shown up and, although he was puffing slightly as we went up the hill and along past Busby's department store, he was keeping pace with Albert all the way; I slogged on, breathing hard, the pack on my back getting heavier by the minute.

Then the unbelievable happened, as it seems to do quite regularly in my life. A large saloon car with powerful lights slid to a halt at the kerb nearby. The window was let down on our side, and a man's cheerful voice called out: 'Where you for?'

'Ben Rhydding,' Albert answered proudly, hitching his giant rucksack up on his back.

'I'm going through to Ilkley – get in, the three of you.'

Albert and Oscar looked at each other in some consternation. After all, the Midnight Hike had been a private dream for weeks. I prayed, earnestly. And I think the patron saint of travellers must have been up late and listening, because Albert suddenly decided this was too good a chance to miss, and we could have all the hiking we wanted on our way back at the end of our week.

'Ta very much. Go on, Les – you first.'

We were at the camp-site well within the hour.

There we struck a snag. The field was inky-black at one

o'clock in the morning, and we had no means of illumination to see where or how to fix the tents.

'Ne'er mind.' Albert was never vanquished. 'We'll roll that big groundsheet out and doss down on that till it gets light.'

'O.K.' But Oscar sounded dubious. 'Looks like it's gunna rain, though.'

And rain it did, as soon as we pulled the blankets up under our chins. It soon developed into a cold and relentless downpour, and we had to gather our goods and chattels together hastily and scramble for shelter under some trees at the far side of the field.

Throughout history, dawn has never been so long in coming. My eyes were dried up and sticking out on cornstalks when eventually first light struck across the leaden skies.

Albert and Oscar worked like trojans to erect the pair of tents and stow away all we had brought with us. I drove in the occasional peg and held things steady, while they coped with all the more technical tasks, tying knots and inserting poles like a couple of fairground experts. At long last the three of us snaked into the sleeping-tent and stretched out on the thin groundsheet, absolutely whacked out. I slept in the middle.

I suppose we were comatose for about an hour and a half before our little canvas world quite suddenly and literally collapsed round our ears.

'Flaming hell!' Oscar had a vivid turn of phrase, and was not as much under the reforming influence of Eastbrook Hall as my brother and I were. 'What the bloody hell's happened?'

We soon found out, when we began to extricate ourselves with difficulty from dripping folds of canvas, obstructive tent-poles and loose guide-lines. One of the farmer's cows had decided to investigate this intrusion by night into its grazing-patch. I tried to make friends with it – I think possibly it was the first cow I had ever seen at really close quarters – but Albert and Oscar would have none of that, and chased it off to a distant corner of the field. And then we raised our shelters from the dead and set them firm and steady all over again, before deciding we were too hungry to sleep any more, and having a makeshift but very consoling breakfast.

During the Sunday morning we went over to the stone buildings to greet the farmer and his wife and collect our pint of fresh milk. They were very good to us, offered every assistance and loaned us several household items we had either forgotten or had not thought to bring with us. Remembering my partiality, Albert told the farmer's wife he would pay her threepence if she would make me a rice pudding during our stay. She promised faithfully to do so, and would not hear of taking any money for it. In fact she made three during our visit, which we all shared. And I may say they were a great help in keeping body and soul together during that essentially frugal week.

After an early tea we walked the two miles to Burley, where my brother had promised to meet friends from the Eastbrook camp at the little Methodist chapel for evening service. How he and Oscar kept their spirits and energy going after the night we had endured, I shall never know. For myself, I was dead on my feet. All I remember of the proceedings is keeping my eyes fixed on a vase of sweet peas that stood on a table in front of the pulpit, and willing myself to stay awake enough to join in the hymns. While we were standing for these I could just about manage it; but the moment we sat down for the sermon I went fast asleep on Albert's shoulder, and had to be nudged back regularly into a state of glassy-eyed semi-consciousness.

That night, rain or no rain, I slept like a log for nine hours solid.

That September Grandma Riley died in Seaton Street, of rheumatic fever and chronic overwork. I was not allowed to attend the funeral, but they let me call in before the hearse arrived, to bid her a last farewell. She was laid out in her coffin under the single window of the cramped living-room, and no light shone on her because the blind was down in mourning. I looked at her white-shrouded body for a long moment. The shrivelled, yellowish shell of her face bore not the slightest resemblance to the apple-dumpling of a grandma I had known and loved so well, and I was very taken aback by it.

I had seen death before, but never that of a loved one and at such close quarters.

'Get back to school, Les,' my dad ordered me quietly. 'No place for young lads, this.' Mum slumped near the coffin, sobbing softly into a white hanky; I don't think she even realised I was there. Grandad Riley sat straight-backed and frozen-faced, like some sort of statue. But the tears were running down his cheeks and, if he knew, he made no attempt to wipe them away.

As I left the house, the strong smell of white windsor soap came wafting from the open kitchen door. Outside, in her tiny patch of garden Grandma's flowers lived on, though she had gone. The rain glistened on antirrhinums, scarlet and gold, standing to attention like guardsmen. I clambered back on my bike and free-wheeled down the passage as silently as I could. Once in the street, I picked up speed and went racing thankfully back to school.

My brother Albert was miles away, slaving his heart out at Hardaker and Sons. They didn't let you off your apprenticeship duties in those days for something as trivial as a grandma's funeral; not even if, as a babe in arms, you had lain in your cot and watched her little yellow bird fall off its perch and perish.

Oh, no. 'There's no sentiment in business, lad,' they were fond of saying. 'Just get on with the job – and thank the Lord you've got one.'

The Lord seemed very far away from both of us, that solemn day.

Chapter Seven

❖

Good evening, Mr Priestley

A week before my grandma died, I had been enrolled as a pupil at the secondary school Albert had left behind a year before. Now called Hanson High, this big and imposing building was built in 1897, and together with the nearby St Clement's Church it dominated the upper half of Barkerend Road. It catered for about six hundred boys and a roughly equal number of girls, who occupied a separate half of the school and were rarely glimpsed by us except when they were showing themselves off through the heavy railings that separated our playgrounds, or dashing in strictly supervised groups along shared corridors to their separate classrooms.

The school had a notable history. In February 1870, W.E. Forster (the M.P. for Bradford from 1861 to 1886, after whom Forster Square had been named) introduced into Parliament his renowned Education Act; and this became the law of the land six months later. By the Act, school boards were first established. It must have given Forster great gratification that the Bradford School Board administered his Act so well in the years to come that Bradford attained national recognition as a pioneer in the educational field. The Education Act allowed literacy to become available for the first time to all children, however poor their circumstances might be. The Church schools (which had hitherto shouldered the burden of enlightening the masses) were to continue, but where provision was insufficient the school boards were to be elected by all ratepayers, with the power to provide elementary schools out of the rates. The Mayor of Bradford formed the very first school board: there were to be fifteen seats on it and among those elected was James Hanson, a printer, nominated by the working men of the town. Hanson Board School was called after him, and was later to become in turn Hanson Secondary, Hanson High and finally Hanson Grammar School.

Naturally I knew little of all this when I was accepted on that bright, smoky, September day into Form 2a and shepherded, along with all the other newcomers, into the Assembly Hall to be addressed by the headmaster, Charles G. Davies. He was a medium-sized, squat pedagogue with short, wispy, dark hair and a pair of gold-rimmed glasses, behind which pale blue eyes had a fixed basilisk stare that never varied throughout the seven years I knew him. Charlie Davies, as he was universally known, was a force to be reckoned with, and he and I were to cross swords dramatically in the later stages of my school career; but on that faraway morning in 1932, with its new surroundings, its air of now belonging to something important, its giving-out of timetables and introduction to form-rooms and its sheer thrill of treading where Albert had trodden before me, Charlie Davies was, quite simply, God.

Hanson High School was run on the principles of discipline, hard work and loyalty, and I loved it from first day to last. My new school cap with the red cross of Appleton House on its crown was a prized possession, and I wore it everywhere. Indeed I think it was the only headgear I have ever regularly adopted, apart from the blue forage-cap that was my regulation adornment for five years in the Royal Air Force. I longed for a school blazer with the embroidered badge on its top pocket proclaiming Hanson's motto, *Age Quod Agis*, but our family could not afford anything like that.

Money seemed to be scarcer than ever that autumn and if Mum managed to get two pounds out of Dad's club earnings at the week's end, that could be deemed a lucky week indeed. Apart from this, she had only the five shillings of Albert's apprentice pay; and with five of us to feed and clothe it was often more than difficult for her to make ends meet. So she

Hanson School and St Clement's Church.

Photo: Author's collection

went out charring, taking her four-year-old son Bill with her, and for some time worked regularly at a second-hand garment shop at the town end of Barkerend Road.

Even that did not always suffice. My parents had various hire-purchase commitments (the upright Underwood piano, the two-valve Marconi wireless-set and my Raleigh Super Sports among them) and the debts began to mount. Throughout her life my mother had a horror of owing money, and one of her darkest days was when The Summons arrived. It was from the City Council, it was on blue paper and it threatened distraint unless the arrears in respect of domestic rates were paid off forthwith. That afternoon, my mother made a parcel of my father's only decent suit and took it to a pawnbroker's called Toothill's in Leeds Road. She then went straight down to the Town Hall to try and settle the matter.

'Are we straight, then?' Dad asked her that evening, as thoughts and fears of sitting on orange-boxes round a paraffin-lamp flew through my mind.

'Straight enough. They're not going to take us furniture, anyroad.'

Mum and Dad.   *Photo: Author's collection*

'Rotten buggers. We've all done us best. You can't get blood out of a stone.' My father's anger at the current situation was deep and unremitting, and increased with every passing year of his unemployment. Then a thought struck him. 'You can't have got that much on the suit? That Toothill's a skinny old devil ... '

'No.' And my mother lowered her eyes to the hands that were clasped in her lap.

'What else?' You could never fool my father where money was concerned – nor any of the Sandses, come to that.

Mum looked up at him, biting her lip. Then she raised her left hand for him to see. The third finger was bare. My father frowned at it, his lips tightening to a thin line.

'Not your wedding ring, lass?'

'We've nowt else, Albert.'

That winter I moved up into the adult section of the Public Library, and now patronised the East Ward branch at the bottom of Seymour Street. My taste had veered away from schoolboys' adventure stories and I was beginning to read more serious stuff, collections of short stories and the odd novel, if the titles took my fancy.

It was nearing closing-time one night when my eyes still roamed the gaslit shelves in search of something substantial to help me while away the long, dark evenings. They lighted on a book I had heard and read about, called *The Good Companions*.

J.B. Priestley was a local man of my father's generation, who had been brought up over on the opposite and somewhat posher side of town, somewhere near Duckworth Lane. His father was a schoolteacher, and quite early on in life he had decided to become a famous author. He sold his first article at the age of sixteen to a London magazine, in 1910. All the portents were there for a brilliant career. After War service in the infantry he went up to Cambridge on an officer's scholarship and then departed for London, where he set out to make his mark. His first and probably his greatest success came with the publication of this book, a long, picaresque novel about the exploits of a sacked Yorkshire joiner, Jesse Oakroyd, who becomes the mascot and moral support of the travelling concert-party after whom the novel is named. *The Good Companions* was a sensation that made Priestley's reputation and much of his fortune. The title was everywhere in the early thirties. Aside from the bookstalls, it was used for calendars, cheap, sentimental prints and even to adorn greetings-cards and chocolate-boxes. Priestley could never make any public appearance without being introduced as 'our own very *good companion*, J.B. Priestley', and he confessed to me in later life that he grew to loathe the famous phrase which he had invented and which had brought him international recognition.

But as I stood there in the stuffy confines of the East Ward Public Library, all I knew about J.B.P. was that he had written a rattling good yarn, and that Bradford as a whole now rather disliked him for deserting his home ground for pastures new 'Down South'. I took the book out, though it was far beyond my usual length and I was sure I should rapidly get bored with it, and carried it home.

It was a revelation to me. Priestley's command of narrative, his gift of characterisation, his descriptive powers and graphic mastery of dialogue made a votary of me, and I have retained an admiration for his work as a popular writer to this day.

My father, who was not given to long novels and preferred his paper and his *Thriller* magazine, agreed I should read it but damned its author with faint praise, just as most of Bradford did because of his seeming desertion. 'J.B. Priestley, aye. Clever chap, that, but a bit big for his boots.' Albert, on the other hand, though he himself was far too busy for serious reading, applauded my choice and told me I might well learn some useful lessons from Priestley's work. 'He can handle words, Les – and he's got his head screwed on right.'

When my wife and I had the honour of becoming friends of the Priestleys in the years that followed, J.B. once told me of an experience of his which typified his home-town's indifference to him, even at the very height of his fame.

I hadn't been in Bradford for a long while, and I went back there to attend a reunion. I'd done it all by then – books, plays, films, even the Postscripts, the lot. I'm standing in this bus-shelter and it's raining. Well, it would be in Bradford, wouldn't it? Bottom of Thornton Road it was, and there's this little frog of a chap in a raincoat, giving me a right up-and-downer. Raining cats and dogs, I remember. Then he sort of sidled up to me and spoke out of the corner of his mouth. 'It's J.B. Priestley, isn't it?' he said; and I thought, 'Fame at last ... even in Bradford.' So I grinned at him. 'Yes,' I said, 'It is.' He looked me up and down again and then said, 'Aye. I thought it must be.' And he moved off to the far end of the shelter, to get away from me. That's Bradford for you.'

Nonetheless, they gave him the freedom of the city; but they made him wait for it until he was well into his eighties.

Alfie Lister, my friend who lived beyond the wall that separated their yard from ours, had the best guider in the neighbourhood. Guiding-carts, or 'guiders' as they were always known, were the ancestors of the modern go-kart. To make your guider (and they were always home-made and never sold in shops) you needed a couple of short planks of stout wood tongued and grooved together to make a reliable platform, and two pairs of serviceable wheels, usually recovered from some old pram or former guiding-cart. The front pair of these swivelled to provide the steering, and this was controlled by a length of thick cord or stout mill-band. Some guiders even had the refinement of an old cushion tacked or nailed to the rear section of the seat, which provided suitable shock-absorption during the guider's progress down hills that had a roughly cobbled surface; this padding marked you out as an owner-driver of some distinction. Alfie's guider had the lot and, to crown all, had been carefully painted in many hues. Its wheels and axles were always greased, and nobody had more careful consideration for, or pride of ownership in, his chosen method of transport than Alfred Lister. Going up hills, the guider would be dragged by one of us while the other sat on the cushion in solitary splendour; going down them, the oak platform could comfortably accommodate both, with Alfie doing the steering and me revelling in the comfort of the padding. The rich might have their Hispano-Suizas, their Lagondas and their Alfa-Romeos, but Alfred and I had the guider – and that was more than good enough for us.

On a lovely summer day in 1933, during the long school holidays (an extravagant six weeks, compared with the measly four we had been granted in junior school), Alfie and I decided to take the guider up to Fagley Woods. This local beauty spot some two or three miles away was noted for two outstanding attractions among the juvenile population of Barkerend Road and Bradford Moor. First, in springtime it was ablaze with bluebells, which we gathered in great profusion for our flower-starved mothers. Second, on the rising waste-ground at the far end of Fagley Woods were two quarries, where limestone had been hewn out for the people's use long years before. One of these was two hundred feet deep, and had a pool of water in the bottom; and it was our boyish pleasure to sprawl out on our stomachs, full-length, and crawl to the very edge, to gaze down wonderingly into the distant depths below. Then we would send gobs of spit curling down through what seemed the vastnessess of space until, if they did not disintegrate on the way, they hit the surface of the water and made a tiny white spurt which always gave us great delight. We would bet with cigarette-cards on who would attain the most hits out of a count of ten. When all this palled, you went on to the other quarry. This was shallower, being only about sixty feet deep, but had the advantages of a sheer drop at one end to be gazed over and a sloping side facing it, where you could clamber down a rough path and play Cowboys and Indians or Foreign Legion on the rock-littered floor. The quarries were a lasting joy to the local lads and lasses, and we all made pilgrimages to them at a least once every summer.

124

Alfie and I spent our regulation half-hour at the major excavation, and did all our spitting until we were dry in the mouth; and then we passed on to explore its minor neighbour. Naturally we went to the deep and sheer end, and tried more expectoration there. But by now our supplies of saliva were somewhat limited and we had not thought to bring a pop-bottle of water with us to replenish them. However, the smaller quarry had other interesting features to be enjoyed, one of which was a tall mast of ancient timber which must have been used in the old days for hauling material up from the base. This soared some twenty or thirty feet aloft, into the clear blue sky. It was gnarled but sound; and it had the handy aid to climbing of metal pins, rusty but fairly reliable, protruding from each side at irregular intervals. The historic pillar stood some six feet or so away from the edge of the quarry, and seemed to be buried timelessly in immovable rock.

'Lets climb it,' Alfie suggested, his eyes shining.

I have never been any kind of hero, having always had the healthiest respect for my own skin, so 'Catch me!' I told him. '*You* can, lad; I've got more sense.'

'S'easy.'

'Go on, then. Tell you what, I'll clap you when you get up there.'

Alfie rummaged in his trouser pockets, which contained every juvenile requirement from the obligatory pen-knife and string to marbles, half-eaten sweets and a piece of coloured chalk. I think it was pink. Anyway, Alfie flourished this in front of me and calmly announced: 'I'm going up that bloody pole, right to t'top. And I'm gunna write me initials up there, just to prove it.'

'Best o' luck,' I said, and parked the guider, upside-down, some yards away from the dangerous edge.

Alfie stood back, hands on hips, and considered his challenge with all the care and coolness of an Everest-scaler studying his final approach to the summit. His gingery hair was tousled, his snub nose set at a determined tilt, and his freckled face was a mask of intrepidity.

'I'll put yours on as well, if you like.'

125

'What?'

'Initials.'

It was a blatant cheat, but I could not resist the temptation. 'Right – let's see you.'

Alfie walked slowly to the mast, gave it a resounding kick, embraced it with both arms and slowly started on his ascent, clawing and clambering with the aid of the side-supports. Half-way up, one of these was loose. He yanked it free of its mooring and tossed it contemptuously to the ground.

'Mind yer head!'

But he did not look down. We young Bradfordians knew the perils of that, having learned this initial climbing skill from our many conquests of the piles of wool-bales outside the mills and warehouses of our sooty town.

Finally Alfie reached the very top, as he had vowed. He clung there precariously with his left arm, while his right extracted the pink chalk from his pocket.

'I'm doing it!'

'Champion.' Then I waited. Would he remember?

'I'm putting yours on now, Les. Can you see?'

I craned my neck, but Alfie's own head and shoulders blocked my view.

'No – I'll just go back a bit.'

I retreated a mere two or three steps, still looking up and hoping to see 'L.S.' appear in pink-chalked capitals. All at once the ground vanished from beneath my feet, and I went over the edge of the quarry backwards.

As I whirled down through the void I had a brief and crazy impression that I was sinking back into some cavity about the size of a shell-hole, or into some strange, soft, greenish-coloured canopy. This was a merciful mental aberration, for had I realised I was actually falling down the quarry I think I would have died in mid-air from shock. Then there was a very nasty crunch as I hit the bottom, and passed out.

When Dad and Albert went over the scene the next day (separately, because Dad would naturally want to go on his own and Albert was taking Doris Langley, whom he was now courting) they concluded in a following discussion that I had

had a narrow escape from early extinction. The drop was a sheer one of at least sixty feet, on to hard and jagged bricks and stones. Had I landed on my head, it would certainly have been smashed in; had I landed awkwardly on my back, that might have been shattered; had I landed in one or two other unlucky ways, I could have broken my limbs and possibly my neck. As it was, I must have done some kind of back-somersault as I flew through the air, for I came to ground on my hands and knees, afterwards banging my head violently as it was flung forward by the impact. This was worked out carefully from the various injuries I had sustained.

I don't know how long I was out for the count. But when I came to, I was indeed huddled on crumpled hands and knees, my face buried in dust and debris. I could hear Alfie shouting out my name from somewhere above, and tried to shout back.

'Les! Where are you?'

'I'm here,' I heard a strange and quavering voice answer. 'Down the quarry ...'

'You're having me on. Come on, it's time we were getting back.' Alfie sounded scared out of his wits.

It took several more yells from me to convince him that I was not pretending, and finally his worried face appeared over the brink, far above.

'Bloody hell! Hang on, I'll bring the guider down.' And he moved away out of sight.

I staggered to my feet somehow, and leaned against the quarry-wall to wait for him. Blood was streaming from a deep wound in my right temple, and more disgusting gore oozed unpleasantly from a large hole in the flesh above my right knee. My legs felt as thin as a spider's, and ached abominably when I tried to move them. Worst of all though were my concussed arms. Although I didn't know it at the time they must have taken almost the full force of my landing, and they hung from my shoulders numb and absolutely useless.

Alfie brought his trusty guider down the sloping end of the quarry and dragged it across the stones to where I floundered in a daze, waiting for him. Somehow he got me on to it and then towed me by brute force up the rough incline on the other side. Then began the long and painful journey up the lane through Fagley Woods. Half-way along, we came to a shop and some little cottages. A man was standing at the open door of one of them, in his shirt-sleeves.

'Nah then – what you two been up to?'

'It's not me, it's me pal,' Alfie explained, more than a little breathless after his exertions. 'He fell down the quarry.'

'Come inside. Hey – leave that guider out there, it's all mucky wi' blood.'

They took me indoors, and the man and his wife washed and cleansed my wounds as best they could. They had an old sticking-plaster which they used to patch up my head, but could find no bandages for my other wounds; so he took a large pocket-handkerchief from a sideboard-drawer, and bound it round my leg above the knee to try and staunch the flow.

'Hospital job, this looks like.'

My usual horror of doctors and medical attention swept over me. 'No, I – I've got to get home. Me mother'll be looking for me.'

'Where do you live?' the good samaritan asked.

'Garnett Street, me,' Alfie informed him. 'He lives on Grant Street.'

'What, down Barkerend Road?'

'That's right.'

The man turned back to me. 'And what do they call you?'

'Sands.' I had had enough of this and now only wanted out. 'Leslie Sands.'

'I think I know your father. *Bert* Sands – the comedian?'

'Aye.'

'Got any money on you?' he enquired.

'No.'

The man turned back to Alfie, who also shook his head. We didn't have a penny-piece between us; we never had.

'I see.' He felt in his pocket, and gave my pal some coppers. 'Get him up to Killinghall Road and get the bus in. There's a Ledgard due through in about a quarter of an hour for Bradford centre. Tell 'em to put you off as near Garnett Street as they can.'

He and his wife waved us away, with Alfie dragging his load again up the lane and me sprawled all over the guiding-cart. I saw there was a patch of fresh blood on the cushion and knew that Alfie would find that hard to forgive.

I never got to know the man's name, but my dad called there the next day on his solitary expedition to the quarry and the coppers were paid back, with interest. I believe they shared a friendly pint at the Royal, Fagley.

Again I was totally incapacitated, and for a couple of weeks spent most of the day on the couch downstairs, reading my books and listening to the wireless. But the doctor didn't have to come this time.

Thanks for the buggy-ride, Alfie.

One day during the same summer holidays, my mother went up to pay one of her usual caring visits to her father Tom Riley, widowed now since the previous September. They say his cry of anguish at finding his wife dead could be heard from the top of Seaton Street to the bottom; and through all the intervening months of his bereavement he had mourned her inconsolably, and seemed like a man lost. All working-men were chauvinists then; he could not cook, and found no pleasure and much difficulty in looking after himself and keeping the house tolerably clean and tidy.

On this occasion, Mum found him slumped in the old rocking-chair, in tears of hopelessness. It moved her greatly and, after cooking him his first decent meal for days and doing some essential washing, she came back home for a serious talk with Dad.

'It's no good, Albert; he can't go on like that.'

'Well he can't come here, lass; we've got no room.'

'There's *three* bedrooms up there – one for him, one for the lads and one for us.'

And after much consideration and chewing of the fat, it was decided we would move lock, stock and barrel to 12 Seaton Street. The rent was four-and-sixpence a week, the rates were bearable, and Grandad Riley would chip in all he could out of his ten shillings a week old-age pension.

Albert and I received the news of the impending transfer with pleasure and a sense of relief. He would be back in the house where he had been born, the neighbourhood was a cut above the slums down Barkerend Road (though it was still composed of stone-built, back-to-back houses) and – an additional bonus – Doris Langley lived in the street that ran parallel, Thursby Street. My mother was thankful that she would be able to take better care of her melancholic father, and in the goodness of her heart never even thought that this might heavily increase the burden she already bore. Dad was non-committal as always: 'Well, we'll have to see.' Mainly, he wanted his Alice to be her usual cheerful self once more. Bill was too young to care much, but rejoiced in the thought that the three of us lads would be sharing the big bedroom, while Dad and Mother would somehow fit a double bed into the medium-sized room over the passage; and Grandad Riley would have the narrow single room between all to himself. He occupied this before we arrived, parting with much of his furniture, but somehow managing to squeeze into his new sleeping-quarters not only his bed and the huge tin box which held all his most cherished possessions, but also a large, black chiffonier complete with china ornaments and stuffed birds in glass cases, that he stubbornly refused to part with in memory of his dear departed wife. The chiffonier and its great overhanging mirror stayed there with him till his dying day. As for me, I greatly welcomed the change, because Seaton Street seemed a lot cleaner than Grant Street had ever done and it was nearer to my beloved school. Added to which, I was pretty confident that since Grandma and Grandad had resided there for most of their married life, Number 12 would be refreshingly free from bedbugs.

It was a crisp and coolish day, but the sun was shining merrily when we did the move. Dad borrowed a handcart from somewhere and his youngest brother, Teddie, helped us to load it up. By this means all our goods and chattels were transported in several journeys through the cobbled streets to our new home, without a penny piece being laid out in removal expenses; though Dad and Teddie did get a little drunk that night, in celebration.

The yard was tiny compared with the one we had left behind, but after all that had accommodated three families instead of two. There were four outside lavatories in the stone wall facing the two houses at the rear, and wooden railings ran across the top of the middens dividing us from the back of Thursby Street, which was on a slightly higher level. But whereas at Grant Street we had looked out on the middens and the tall, red-brick wall that separated us from Barkerend Mills, here we could glimpse the rear houses of the next street, and greet neighbours as they went about their own yards. And to top all, we had a gas-lamp of our very own; it was situated on the Thursby Street side, I grant you, but when night came it shone down benignly on Number 12's new occupants and their next-door neighbours, the Steels at Number 14.

The passage to the street was stone-flagged and had a strip of cobbles down the centre. This was a great improvement on the dark and rough one I had known since I was born. When you went down to the bottom of the passage and levered yourself up on Mrs Palframann's wall in Seaton Street, you could see most of the other side of the city when the weather was clear. You could even catch a glimpse of the Town Hall clock, as it stood in solemn splendour at the bottom of Bradford's bowl.

I remember sitting on the wall that evening and gazing down at the central buildings. Then I slowly looked all the way round the horizon. What you could see of it seemed to be composed entirely of dirty mill-stacks, most of which were everlastingly belching smoke. Over Bradford itself in those days there always hung a pall of this, circular in shape, blackly funereal and to me very threatening. Squatting there, I tried to count all the mill-chimneys I could see. This proved to be quite impossible. There were so very many of them that I soon lost count, and had to give up.

Is this it, I wondered? When I leave school at sixteen, will this still be it? Will this be it for ever? Or will I find a way out – somehow – someday – ?

You've only got one life to live, I thought, and there must be more to it than the mills, the cobblestones and that damned ring of suffocating smoke.

Looking north over the Wool Exchange from City Hall c.1920.

Photo: Christopher Pratt

Chapter Eight

❖

A Good Time Coming –

There's a good time coming,
Be it ever so far away –
That's what I say to meself, says I,
Jolly good luck, hooray!

So ran a popular cheer-up song of the mid-thirties, often played by the popular Jack Hylton and his Orchestra on the radio. In sober truth, 1934 was for Britain one of the worst years this country has ever known.

The so-called 'National Government' was in power. After the disastrous Labour administration of 1929–1931, Ramsay MacDonald had deserted his party to head this forlorn conglomeration, which included many dispirited Right-wingers in its ranks. A somewhat confused election followed, in which the Labour Party lost five-sixths of its seats. In effect, national government never materialised, but national disillusion and unrest lost no time in coming. And in this jolly-good-luck year of 1934, J.B. Priestley made his *English Journey*, to find huge stretches of the kingdom reduced to poverty, apathy and disenchantment. In Jarrow, two men out of three were unemployed; and conditions in the Rhondda were so intolerable as to beggar even his powers of description.

The infamous Household Means Test had been introduced in 1931, and after three years of application was having its fullest deadly effect. By this detestable measure the earnings, savings and any other assets whatsoever of all members of the family were assumed to be available to support the head of the household, should he be out of work. Some of the results of the Means Test were truly appalling. Families broke up in despair, sending their children into official care or into the dubious security of adoptive parenthood, and selling up their few possessions to stem the rising tide of debt; but still in many cases they ended up homeless and destitute. Some husbands and fathers, losing all hope, threw up their responsibilities and simply walked out, going 'on the road' or (if they were older and incapacitated) 'on the parish', the senior Yorkshireman's euphemism for the solitude and desolation of the workhouse. 'Jolly good luck – hooray!'

At home, the domestic situation mirrored the national despondency. The hopes we had all cherished of a happier life in Seaton Street had failed to materialise. Having moved into another man's house, Dad felt he was no longer king of the midden, and he was a proud man. His growing sense of inferiority was accentuated by more than five years now of odious unemployment. Consequently, we hardly ever saw him in the evenings for he would be either down at his mother's, airing his troubles, or circulating among the many public-houses in the area. Grandad Riley, whose house we now felt we had invaded summarily, was becoming more and more unsteady on his pins, and thumped off only once or twice a week to free us from his attempted domination and call on old pals, or perhaps to have the odd game of dominoes over a half-pint of mild-and-bitter at the Adelphi Inn in Leeds Road. My brother Albert took all this philosophically, was friends with everyone and regularly cut Grandad's hair in its customary convict's style to save the old man the expense of a visit to the barber's. In the middle of all this, my slaving and miraculous mother contrived to feed and dress her five male charges on the most limited of means, to maintain an unfailing cheerfulness and to keep the peace amongst us as best she could. It is small wonder that my dad finally christened her 'The Indiarubber Woman'.

This was the year my Grandad Sands died, and Grandma Sands was left on her own to run her little empire down in

Barkerend Road. Twelve months before that they had moved next door to Number 196, a house and shop owned by a thriving brewery, and therefore always kept in a good state of maintenance and repair. Here they had a vast and cavernous bedroom over the shop, where Grandma Sands (now a bulky fifteen or sixteen stone) commandeered the best position in a large double bed that projected from the centre of one wall. My poor weasel of a grandad, now thoroughly under the fleshy thumb of his more forceful spouse, was relegated to a narrow single bed directly under the ill-fitting window, whose rattling frame permitted the entry of cold and bone-chilling draughts. I think he meant to refer to this unenviable situation as being like the Alps, but the word he came out with was 'Avalanches'.

'She'll finish me off for good Les, now she's put me in the bloody Avalanches. Never mind, she'll get a good trip to Morecambe out of the insurance. She's got me well covered, you know. Never covered herself. Well, she wouldn't would she? I mean, somebody else 'ud be drawing it!'

After he had gone, it seemed to me that the sharp smell of newly tanned leather lingered on and on in the space where his cobbler's bench had once stood. The shop has changed hands many times since then; but when I was last in there a couple of years ago, I could still smell that tang. Or I thought I could.

Somehow, in the middle of that year of near-despair in Bradford, a new interest full of colour and variety came my way.

The *Telegraph and Argus* was at that time running a children's club that rejoiced in the name of the 'Nignogs'. If you were to use that term nowadays in a public place, you might well find yourself up in front of some kind of Racial Discrimination Board; but in those days it was completely innocuous. You sent off a shilling or so to their premises in Hall Ings and this brought you by return a handsome membership-card and a tasteful little badge, enamelled in royal blue and gold, that depicted a small, pixie-like head with 'Nignog' bannered underneath. This badge was worn by schoolkids all over Bradford who daily read their special column in the paper, and indulged in many worthy Nignog activities such as competitive sports and works for local charities. Once a year these culminated in the presentation on the Alhambra Theatre stage, for one week only, of the locally-famed *Nignog Revue*. One of the lads at Hanson, Geoffrey Hudson, was their leading comic, and used to tear the house down with his annual portrayal of the check-suited, bowler-hatted and dim-witted Yorkshire tyke, 'John Willie'.

I saw auditions for the Revue advertised and so, one dank and misty evening, I tucked some of my father's sheet-music under my arm and went down to Hall Ings to try my luck.

The auditions were held in the employees' recreation-room on an upper floor of the *Telegraph and Argus* building and were conducted, under the aegis of the paper's editor F.H. Timperley, by a professional producer called Arnold Tolson. I can see Mr Tolson now, pudgy and sallow, with a bard's haircut streaming out behind his high and sweat-beaded forehead, as he first organised in a soft but compelling voice the crowd of young hopefuls and their pushy parents into some semblance of order; and then listened to each juvenile attempt at entertainment with the same amount of interest and patience, whether or not it merited such careful and professional attention. The upright piano, which seemed to me to have a very beery twang to it, was somewhat out of tune, but the wild-haired lady who thumped its keys did so with a bright and enthusiastic smile which encouraged every aspirant to give of his or her very best.

For some time I stood with others, near the full-sized billiards-table at one end of the room, and watched my fellow-hopefuls as they went through their varied paces. We had dancers, singers, reciters and even a diminutive and dextrous conjurer, who wore a Belle Vue blazer and had bright red hair. It crossed my mind that Belle Vue was the secondary school that my hero J.B. Priestley had attended in the far past.

And then it was my turn. I handed my dad's sheet-music of *Atchoo!* over to the lady with the bright smile, and did my utmost to emulate his always-superb rendering of that comic number. It told of a young man who suffered from a perpetual cold, and of the troubles this brought him during his courtship, wedding and somewhat disastrous married life. The refrain ran:

> *All that he could say was 'A – a – atchoo,*
> *A-a-atchoo …. a-a-atchoo,'*
> *There he sat till he froze*
> *Making love to her through his doze; (wait for laugh)*
> *She cried 'Jim, the lights are dim,*
> *Love me like you used to do …*
> *Say something sweet and sloppy, dear,'*
> *He said 'I would, lass, but I f-f-f-fear*
> *I'm gunna sneeze – again – it's coming – it's here!*
> *A-a-a-a-a- ATCHOO!!!'*

Whatever you may think of it now, it got me the job; and I became second comic in that year's edition of the *Nignog Revue.*

The six or seven weeks of rehearsal were a joyous period for me, as I learned all manner of things connected with appearing for the first time on the large stage of a proper theatre. Arnold Tolson, with immeasurable forbearance, taught us how to stand still with some semblance of repose when not in the immediate focus of attention, how to move easily and confidently about the stage, what to do with our arms and hands, and how to project effectively across a sixteen-hundred-seater auditorium. The choreographer Val Lorraine, in her little studio at the top of Manchester Road (called modishly enough 'Beacon House', after the pedestrian crossings recently established by Hore-Belisha), instructed us in the rudiments of tap-dancing, the erect carriage of head and shoulders, the loosened lower limbs, the double-shuffle and the buck-and-wing. I was lucky to be a member of a most talented company which included, in addition to many outstanding 'principals', two whole troupes of dancing-girls, one juvenile and one of nubile teenagers. What boy of thirteen could ask for more than to watch the latter team rehearsing night after night, smiling provocatively at you as they kicked their legs high in their skin-tight costumes? I was a growing lad, don't forget.

I played The Showman, who opened the proceedings with a rousing speech; and later in the programme I essayed the roles of Villainous Arab and Lugubrious Feed to Geoffrey Hudson in his renowned *Teacake Sketch*, filled in during numerous other sketches and, of course, contributed my loud singing-voice and clumsy attempts at tap-dancing to the chorus-numbers.

In one of the offerings I was part of a trio of juvenile 'acrobats', who performed cod antics in which most of the tricks went wrong. This climaxed in the smallest member hoisting me up on his shoulders, where I strutted and preened amidst applause from 'out front'. The audience was not to know that my ascent and apparently secure position were assisted by a flying-wire and a cumbersome body-harness; and when a pretty girl 'waitress' in short skirt and black stockings walked across the stage, my supportive companion, encouraged by her ogling, dashed off into the wings after her and left me hanging high and dry. Wait for laugh, and then blackout! You see? I was picking up the terminology already.

During the later rehearsals, the Producer told me I must wear something called a 'jock-strap' to protect my middle from the stresses and strains of the body-harness, and I thought it most kind of him when he offered to entertain me at his digs and select an appropriate fit from the large selection he apparently kept there. The tea and toasted teacakes his landlady whistled up were delicious, and he entranced me for an hour with his tales of the professional theatre and his former triumphs as an actor in the provinces. He had actually once played Mr Wu in *The Chinese Bungalow* at Sheffield! In due course came the all-important fitting, which seemed to take an unconscionable time and consisted mainly of his whispered encouragements and gentle fumblings with my private parts, as he sought to adjust the tight-fitting elastic straps and the woven pouch of this curious piece of equipment. I was red with embarrassment throughout, and was glad when I made my escape into the fresh air and drizzle of Horton Lane. The Producer, apparently disappointed in my responses, never gave me tea and teacakes again; nor did he ever make any attempt to repeat this performance, surely one of the least distinguished of his long career.

THE
BRADFORD TELEGRAPH & ARGUS
NIGNOG CLUB

The author as he appeared in the programme for the 1934 Nignog Revue at the Alhambra Theatre. *Photo: Author's collection*

At long last the Monday came when we were to open for the week at the Alhambra; and I woke up with a high temperature and a miserable croak in my throat where my voice should have been. I honked at Dad that I would never be able to get over my important introductory lines as The Showman in this state. Resourceful as ever, he went round to see Mrs Watson the herbalist, and came back with a small phial of something called 'Syrup of Squills and Chloric Ether'. This I regularly poured down my gullet throughout the day. My incapacity caused some concern at the dress rehearsal, but I was allowed to go on as planned in the evening. (There was no alternative because the revue, being an amateur concern, carried no understudies.) When my entrance came, shortly after curtain-up, I walked boldly on to the stage and tried to captivate the packed house with my stirring speech of welcome. The lines were there all right, but the necessary ringing tones were conspicuous by their absence. All I could summon up was a deep, hoarse croaking, reminiscent of a frog with laryngitis. Although the content of my speech must have been unintelligible to the majority, at least I got the first laugh of the evening.

The visitation had miraculously disappeared by the second night, and I can only agree now with the old-stagers who laughed it off as being all due to nerves; nonetheless, my father swore by Syrup of Squills and Chloric Ether for ever afterwards. I must admit I clung to it as a remedy myself until later (in my years of repertory) it became unobtainable and disappeared from my dressing-table, to be replaced by that invaluable voice-aid, Sanderson's Throat Specific.

After its presentation at the town's leading theatre the *Nignog Revue*, in a condensed version, toured hospitals and old people's homes. I was grateful to be included in this pared-down rendering, which gave me the recurring opportunity of singing not one but two of my father's comic songs. They can't have been very suitable offerings from a thirteen-year-old lad to an audience of sickly patients or experienced and hard-bitten senior citizens, but they always seemed to go down well enough, though I never shone with any of Geoff Hudson's luminosity.

One of our visits went as far afield as Morecambe, my grandmother's personal heaven-on-earth, where a new establishment was to be opened called 'The Sunshine Home for the Aged'. Our little concert was to be the high-spot of the inaugural ceremony; and it was on our coach journey there that I learned from our ever-bubbling lady accompanist that the Home would be officially opened by Mr J.B. Priestley.

I stood in the wings of the tiny stage and listened to his sympathetic and subtly humorous speech. He was thick-set and deep-voiced, had a face like crumpled brown paper that hid the most mischievous of grins, and wore a navy-blue, chalk-stripe suit. But I hardly heard a word he said; for all the time I was listening with apparently rapt attention, I was thinking of *The Good Companions* and trying to realise that here, only a yard or so away from me, stood the man who had created them.

He stayed on for our performance, and afterwards sat on an upturned barrel in the wings and talked to us about the theatre and the music-hall (of which he was always a staunch supporter). He had written *Dangerous Corner* by then and a couple of other successful plays into the bargain, as well as keeping up his regular output of the popular novel. It seemed to me, and the opinion has never altered, that here was a giant of our times, and a master of all the things that I was really interested in – the English language, the creation of books and plays, and their interpretation and dissemination. Oh, yes – I went home full of J.B. Priestley that night.

'Aye well,' Grandma Sands said, when I gave her the customary and required account. 'He would be there, that chap. Allus likes to get his name in t'papers.'

News of my stage work spread to Hanson, where the headmaster, Charles G. Davies, was somewhat sour in his reactions and warned me during a private interview in his study that too much extra-mural frivolity might well interfere with the progress of my schoolwork. That, he stressed quite rightly, must always come first.

'You've done Well so far, Sands.' Charlie Davies had a vocal mannerism that told you by the judicious use of pause and emphasis exactly where he felt additional capital letters should be incorporated in a sentence. 'I see by your Report Book you were second at Christmas, and you came out Top of the Form in the summer exams. Don't let it slide, we're expecting Great Things of you.'

Inside myself, I wished them luck.

One cheering point was, and I had Albert's word for this, the teachers at Hanson were all first-rate. The secret of their undoubted success lay in the fact that, without exception, they treated us as minds and not mere mentalities; and they never forgot, even in those dark days of Britain's economic turmoil, that we were not only the sons and daughters of the lost generation – we were also human beings in our own right, who deserved our fair chance in a changing world.

In February 1935 I played my first part in a straight play that somebody else had written. William Cox, the senior English-master, always contributed a short comedy to the annual school concert, which was held over two evenings in St Clement's Church on the opposite side of Barkerend Road. That year the play was called *Grand Partiality*, and was all about a northern suburban family plagued by the fits and foibles of an interfering and cantankerous grandfather. I was favoured with the role of Mrs Spink, the long-suffering Mum of the piece. This, as far as I can recall, was my only appearance ever 'in drag' apart from a character I portrayed much later on in repertory, who had to impersonate a woman in the farce *Will Any Gentleman?* Years later, when I became a National Theatre player, it was mooted that I might be cast as Lady Bracknell in a projected production of *The Importance Of Being Earnest*, to be directed by Jonathan Miller. As far as I know, nothing ever came of this project and, for the sake of both Mr Miller and Oscar Wilde, this is perhaps just as well. But it meant that I never did complete my hat-trick of 'drag' performances.

For the time, Mrs Spink was quite enough to cope with. I felt I never quite measured up, despite the most diligent of application, to Mr Cox's expectations; but I did the best I could, and if nothing else my stage make-up was impeccable,

The author, seated at the table, in his first straight role – Mrs Spink in *Grand Partiality* at St Clement's Church in February 1935.

Photo: Author's collection

thanks to the lore I had picked up in the *Nignog Revue*. It matters not that it was more suited to an end-of-the-pier show than to a suburban living-room: it had five and nine, lake-liner, blue eyeshadow – everything; and I thought it a masterpiece. Which is more than can be said for the wig, which came on hasty hire from Charles Fox in London, fitted where it touched, and resembled nothing so much as a long-abandoned eagle's nest.

School had now become the most important thing in my life. Not only did it provide knowledge and instruct in its use; it also gave scope for all kinds of fringe activities, to quicken our minds and broaden our young horizons. There was always a function of some kind being organised or taking place. The school concerts and the various parties (end-of-term, Christmas, and the like) gave me valuable training in the development of stage presence and taught me gradually how best to put myself over to a live audience. There were Sports Days, Swimming Galas, the

Debating Society, mock parliaments and pastimes to suit every taste, academic and athletic. I slowly came to realise that I was enjoying myself and learning, all at the same time.

Some things I would rather not have learned, but they came my way just the same.

One of our masters was known to his intimates (and I use the term advisedly) as 'Gaffer'. He was a good teacher and well-liked, but there was one side of him that was always kept carefully hidden during school hours.

Gaffer was a homosexual, the first true homosexual I ever met. There were to be many others as the years went by; and one or two of them (although I never shared their proclivities) would be numbered among my greatest friends. An illegitimate son, Gaffer lived on the other side of Bradford in what he chose to describe as 'my auntie's house'. This lady was actually his natural mother, though I didn't gain this knowledge until years after I had known him. He seemed to have ample money to provide small treats and luxuries for his pets and, strangely enough, if you were invited to spend an evening over at Gaffer's you were usually the envy of those you confided in. There you would be regaled with chocolates, the occasional beer and a vast amount of risqué stories, before the real business of the night began. Gaffer would eventually undo your flies and proceed to enjoy himself, whether you liked it or not.

I don't know why he singled me out for a special treat, as my responses were usually very half-hearted. I must admit though that I allowed him to caress me at will and showed none of my distaste, because I was very fond of him as a personal guru, and also as an individual and striking personality. It seemed to me his sense of humour made up for many of his shy-making shortcomings. But Gaffer came to my house one night and asked my parents if he might take me away on a brief holiday to Blackpool, explaining that he knew times were hard for us and was only trying to help people less fortunately placed than himself. All unsuspecting, my father and mother agreed to a suggestion that was put forward with every last ounce of his customary gentleness and charm.

Blackpool in any case was a magnet to me. I had always loved its breeziness and devil-may-care spirit, the sweep of its promenade and the Golden Mile, the Tower, the Big Wheel, the theatres and pier shows, and the general air of sheer, unalloyed enjoyment that pervaded all.

We stayed at a small private hotel on the front, not far from the Central Pier. Gaffer had booked a large room at Blenheim Mount, with two single beds. The food was first-rate as far as I could tell, and on top of that there was the delight of having the use of a proper and well-appointed bathroom. I think this was the greatest single pleasure on that holiday, for up until then I had been used to tin baths in front of the fire, filled by kettles and ladling-cans of hot water from the range boiler; and later (when puberty made privacy desirable) to somewhat irregular visits to the Swimming and Slipper Baths, up Leeds Road. So during my three or four days at Blenheim Mount I took full advantage of the high-class ablutionary facilities there. And, I believe for the first time in my life, I used scented toilet soap. Lux.

Gaffer played his cards well, and for the first two days we had little physical contact apart from the odd stroke or tickle. Instead, we exploited to the full the treats that a sunny, crowded Blackpool had to offer. I remember a popular song of the time was *Have You Ever Been Lonely?* With Gaffer, there was never any chance of that. We revelled in the antics of Syd Seymour and his Mad Hatters Band on the North Pier, went round the vast Pleasure Beach at the South Shore, and paid a visit to a touring production of *Candida* at the Palace Theatre. One day it would dawn on me that I had been privileged to witness Stephen Haggard's unrivalled portrayal of Marchbanks, the flawless grace of Ann Harding as Candida herself, and the polished technique of Leon Quartermaine as her clergyman husband; but these names meant little to the Bradford lad who watched them at that time. We made the statutory pilgrimage to Uncle Tom's Cabin, a famous pub on the North Shore; and here Gaffer persuaded me into drinking my first gin-and-tonic. Toilet soap and gin-and-tonic! The good times seemed to be coming, at last.

It was on the second night that Gaffer came into my bed and made serious advances, kissing and squeezing and snorting ardently, for he was rather overweight and suffered from a chronic sinus complaint.

I was upset and bewildered but not surprised, and I derived no enjoyment whatever from his attempts at love-making. In some ways I was sorry about this for, as I have said, he was a good friend, he could be good company, and I liked and admired him greatly as a schoolmaster. But when he lay underneath me and asked me, sweating copiously, to pretend he was a woman, I am afraid I found this quite beyond my powers of imagination, and failed him wretchedly.

The third and final night of our short break, I was left alone except for a hurried embrace and a goodnight peck; and I returned to Bradford the following day a sadder but wiser young man. Still, at least I had laughed my head off at Syd Seymour; and, through *Candida*, I had discovered George Bernard Shaw.

The fifth *Nignog Revue* came round at the Alhambra, and again I featured in it. This time I had two principal parts: Prince Oscar, and The Spirit of the Sea. (We had a taste for high romance in those far-off days.) As Geoffrey Hudson was in his matriculation year at school he elected to forgo the delights of stardom; so his successor had to be found for the leading comedy role of 'John Willie'. I asked to be considered and was one of the few, the very few, who were granted an audition. However, the rest of those competing were put to shame by a pocket-sized precocity with a shock of straw-like hair who sang *I'm Knee Deep in Daisies* in an appealingly eccentric, piping voice and did a most accomplished clog-dance. He walked away with the coveted part because he thoroughly deserved to, and when the show was produced was an even greater success in it than Geoffrey Hudson had been. His name was Ernest Wiseman and he was the son of Harry Wiseman, who toured the Northern clubs as half of a double act much like Sands and Grant but known as Johnson and Wise. The diminutive Ernest later auditioned for the B.B.C. personality Brian Michie, and became one of that impresario's 'Discoveries'. He went with Michie's show to London, where he graced a West End stage at the Prince of Wales's Theatre. In the same company was a young up-and-coming comedian called Eric Bartholomew. The two of them found an instant rapport, joined up as a double act in their own right, and went on to fame and fortune as the unforgettable Morecambe and Wise.

Hello again, Ernie; how was it for you?

Chapter Nine

❖

Slogging it Out

After seven long years of unemployment, Dad confessed one day to my brother: 'I've got to get a job, Albert. I'm getting lazy. For a long time now I haven't wanted to work – not *proper* work, I mean – and that's no good to anybody.'

So it was that Bert Sands, whose name as a club comic, along with that of his partner Jack Grant, was now well-established all over the industrial North, went out and got himself what he thought of as a proper job. It took weeks of hard searching, but he came home elated one evening and announced to his Alice: 'I've started, lass; I've started!' His face was grimy, his wiry hair thick with dust and he was wearing a pair of borrowed 'drills', the name we always gave to suits of denim overalls.

'What you doing, Dad?' Bill asked him excitedly. He was now all of eight years old, with a wiry figure, a mop of tousled fair hair and the infectious grin he had inherited from his father.

'I'm doing a man's job, lad. Coal-heaving.'

And then he showed us his hands. They were a mass of open cuts, dark purple bruises and caked coal-dust.

'Get in that kitchen and get them things washed,' my mother commanded him. 'Hot water, mind, from t'kettle. I'll fetch you some disinfectant.'

I remember him whistling merrily as he trotted across the room to do her bidding. Albert remembers, too.

He went off and got himself one of the lousiest jobs he could possibly have tackled, after being out of work for all that time. Filling up sacks of coal, down at the sidings. I'll never know how he managed it! Do you know, I could have wept for him. But he stuck it for about twelve months and it toughened him up again. After that he went off on some demolition work, taking old boilers out and knocking walls down with a sledge-hammer, that sort of thing. 'Course, he *could* work, you know: when he fed properly, he was as strong as a horse.

'Tell you what, Dad,' I said to him one day, 'I bet this is the hardest job you've had since you were born.'

'I wasn't born, lad,' and he winked the Bert Sands wink, 'I was quarried.'

Dad was back in a job anyway, and for a long time the skies were brighter.

Grandma Sands, however, had little faith in the popular conviction that good times were just around the corner.

'Trades's bucking up, Les, and I'm thankful for that. But it's not the first time I've known it. Trade bucked up a lot just before the Great War.'

'Do you think there'll ever be another, Grandma?'

'Nay – that 'ud be telling, wouldn't it?'

For those who could read them, the signs were already more than evident. Mussolini had conquered Abyssinia. In Spain, Franco had raised his revolt against the Republican government. That same year Hitler occupied the formerly demilitarised Rhineland, and the Allies' infamous Appeasement Policy got under way.

I had little concern for international disputes then however, and was jogging on happily with all my school interests and activities.

I was honoured by the senior English-master when he chose me to play the lead in his offering that year at the school concert, an acid little comedy about a confidence-trickster, called *The Shorn Wolf*.

William Cox was one of the most powerful influences on my life; and it all began when I took part in his one-act plays at St Clement's, before we had even met in class as master and pupil. He was of tall and beefy structure, had clean-shaven and weatherbeaten features and wore his M.A.'s gown always with an air of justifiable self-esteem. He came to our house several times on matters of school import, and my father once described him as looking like 'a navvy dressed up in his Sunday best'.

The Shorn Wolf was one of his sharpest comedies and was enthusiastically received at the school concert that February. I played another part before the night was out, that of the leader of the school dance-band – called, that year and for two nights only, 'Hiram Hayseed's Hideous Howlers'.

At Mr Cox's instigation, I went that summer to the School Camp at Stratford-upon-Avon. There was a permanent camping-site along Loxley Road, where bell-tents could be hired in which we occupied borrowed sleeping-bags, fearful of the earwigs that seemed to get everywhere. (But they didn't suck your blood, unlike the bugs of yore.) There were no cooking facilities laid on but we had an open fire in the field, and our hot food was organised by the two supervising masters, Leonard Payling (the junior English-master) and Harold Cocking. There were a lot of stewed prunes and apricots, I remember. There were also serviceable washing facilities, where hot water was plentiful and the showers well-patronised, with their powerful and invigorating sprays. We were there for a whole week, and visited the Memorial Theatre on two magical occasions. The whole holiday cost just thirty-seven shillings and sixpence, all-inclusive.

I sat in the gods next to my current hero, 'Spike' Payling, and can see again in my mind's eye the first professional Shakespeare I ever witnessed. The play was *Julius Caesar*, which we all knew well from our school-readings of the text. Peter Glenville, an actor of note who later became a famous theatre director, was a dark and compelling Antony; I think the Brutus was played by James Dale; and a quite remarkable Cassius was given to us by Donald Wolfit.

William Cox, M.A. – the finest schoolmaster of them all!

Photo: Author's collection

'Watch his eyes,' Spike Payling muttered to me, during the Quarrel Scene. And indeed they were well worth watching. Wolfit, who had been at Nottingham University with Payling, had large and luminous optics which he used to great effect, especially when he was not actually speaking but listening to the other actors. I think I learned then that much of good acting rests in the art of reaction; and the truer and more convincing that reaction can be, the greater will be the effect of the scene as a whole.

I was sixteen that May. For eighteen months I had been doing two paper-rounds, to help out at home and make myself some pocket-money. They were sandwiched in between a very early breakfast and morning school, and brought in six shillings every week. At her decision, this meant four-and-six for my mother, and one shilling and sixpence for myself. 'Oh, you're rolling in it,' Grandma Sands commented, 'But don't let it go to your head!'

With some regret these deliveries had been relinquished, because all my energies had to go into my studies now. In addition to my nine to four-fifteen stint at Hanson, I was working a solid five nights a week towards my matriculation examination. This was the equivalent of the present GCSEs, and its winning was an essential if you were to try and get yourself a 'white collar job'. My heart was wholly set on that, after the stench of hot, wet wool and the clamour of busy looms I had witnessed in my childhood, on the classic occasion of my one and only visit to the mill.

So following the school concert in February, when once again I played in a Bill Cox play and also again led the school dance-band (the star attraction of the evening), I buckled down to work for the June exams. As always, Albert pointed the way. 'Don't come a cropper like I did, Les. You've only got one chance, and this is it. Start swotting at least six weeks before the exam. That's what I should have done, and that's what you're going to do.'

So that's exactly what I did. I concentrated as hard as I knew how in the classroom – it was easier now I didn't keep falling asleep at my desk after my paper-rounds – and carried my studies upstairs with me to our communal bedroom in the evenings. My desk was an old wash-hand-stand in front of the window. My extra notebooks were talked out of the school secretary, who had charge of the stationery store next to the headmaster's study. My pencils were begged, borrowed or stolen from all and sundry. But I did buy myself a fountain-pen. It was a Platignum, its case was mottled blue-and-silver, and it cost me all of half a crown. The bedroom was not warm, and there were many distractions from outside and down below. There was a would-be tenor who lived in the next yard up, a shell-shocked war veteran who was forever belting out Nelson Eddy and Jeanette MacDonald hits like *Sweethearts*, *Rose Marie* and *Ah, Sweet Mystery of Life!* at the top of his powerful voice. One sweet mystery of life to me was why the hell his throat didn't explode, with all the extra pressure he used to put on it. This constant roar did little to assist my assimilation of Palgrave's *Golden Treasury* or further my studies of European History and Parliamentary Government in the Nineteenth Century; but I soon got to know the words of all the songs backwards. The radio would often be blaring out downstairs for Grandad Riley's benefit, and sometimes young Bill would be kicking up hell in the back yard with his pals. But I would close the window tight, light a cigarette if I had one, and shut my mind to these distractions as I went off blithely in the company of Keats, Coleridge and Shelley – or struggled manfully to master the political contrivances of Palmerston, Gladstone and Disraeli.

One day, I swore to myself, I would have a room of my own to work in, one specifically designed for that purpose. All I needed was sufficient space, a steady table, a hard-backed chair, paper and pencil and – above all else – peace and quiet. Nowadays I have a study that is as fine as any I could wish. It is roomy and has all the shelves and cupboards I want. Thickly carpeted, it is furnished in polished mahogany and the finest English leather. (Yes, Grandad Sands, you're here as well.) Its big window looks out on two English rivers, the Severn and the Wye. Its chief bonus is that I can now get all the peace and quiet I need. And yet, sitting here, I sometimes wonder if the quality of the work I do at this imposing desk is any better – though I hope it is not significantly worse – than that I did perched uncomfortably at the old wash-hand-stand at Number 12. It was a true friend to me and, like the Platignum pen I treasured and the pencils I could never bear to discard when they were worn out, is a part of me still.

These solitary sessions in the bedroom brought one notable and quite unexpected benefit. It started with a waving acquaintance with Thursby Street neighbours, who had to come through to their backyards to visit the lavatories which were over the wall above ours and lit by the same gas-lamp that towered over our own. Evelyn Rhodes was older than I was and always had a fancy for my elder brother, who was quite impervious to her somewhat fleshy charms. She was a constant waver. Her elder brother Frank was a waver, too. He had been the secretary of a local cricket club that had recently expired through lack of support. Albert knew them both, of course. He came home one day and told me Frank had inherited a portable typewriter from the secretarial obligations that were no longer in force. He had no use for it now and it was up for sale for five shillings, in cash.

'You ought to have a typewriter, Les. You do a bit of writing, and it could save you time and trouble.'

'But I can't type.'

'You're a Sands, aren't you? You can learn.'

I couldn't manage to raise five shillings, but somehow scraped together half a crown. Spencer Tracy, Alice Faye and the Marx Brothers had to be neglected for a while, but I don't suppose they noticed very much difference. My loyal brother found the balance for me. The Underwood portable came into my bedroom-study and, as a relaxation from school work, I gradually taught myself to become the two-finger typist that I am to this day.

But it wasn't all hard slog. At week-ends I sallied forth with two new and stout friends I had recently made. Tom Pullen, who lived not far from Doris Langley in nearby Thursby Street, was one of the closest friends I have ever had. Tom was a stocky young chap with a head of strawy, Brylcreemed hair that was his pride and joy, and a predilection for thick, gingery, tweed suits. We shared the same oblique sense of humour, and the same investigative interest in the opposite sex. Tom had left school at fourteen and now had a clerking job in a shipping office in central Bradford, concerned with the transit of bulk materials all over Britain. He was a staunch and always entertaining companion, and an accomplished pianist. Jim Kelly lived in Hillside Villas down Barkerend Road, and worked at a large hardware stores along Godwin Street in the centre of the city. Jim was older than Tom and I by a year or so, taller and bulkier, and nearly always wore a gabardine raincoat, tightly belted round his middle. He had a laugh like an amiable hyena, was the best possible audience for the latest funny story and always seemed to have oodles of spending-money, far more in fact than one would have expected from a trainee shop-assistant. This was a matter for our lasting conjecture and Jim's own private satisfaction, for he never breathed a word about its source. Whatever that may have been, we profited frequently and gratefully from his jovial generosity.

On Friday nights, provided I made a stern bargain with myself to catch up with my week's revision on the Saturday morning, we would all go down to the pictures together. (This was of course after my typewriter had been bought and paid for.) Our cinemas were the Odeon in Manchester Road, the Regent in Manningham Lane, the Morley Street Picture House just above the stage door of the Alhambra, and the Savoy in Darley Street. Here we revelled in the early Astaire-Rogers musicals, the Ritz Brothers, Dick Powell and Joan Blondell and, I suppose above all, the great gangster movies of the thirties, with Edward G. Robinson, Cagney, Bogart and the rest of them. Who of my age can ever forget Paul Muni and George Raft in *Scarface*? We caught up with reissues of *Frankenstein* and Bela Lugosi's *Dracula* (to remind me of my first visit to the legitimate theatre), were chilled by *The Cabinet of Doctor Caligari* and Peter Lorre's '*M*', and saw as much as we could of Bing Crosby and Bob Hope in their early triumphs.

Saturday afternoon was our time for the markets. The old Bradford excelled in these. There was the huge covered market in Kirkgate where I bought copies of sheet-music for a penny each, Tom haunted the bookstalls and the benches of counterfeit antiques, and Jim treated us now and again to a ham sandwich made in a bap as big as a pram-wheel. Then – also under glass-roofed cover – there were the Meat Market, the Fish Market and the Fruit Market all to be traversed.

But best of all when the weather was propitious was the Open Air Market, just off John Street. This was always referred to by older and wiser citizens as the 'Quack Market'. Here, Bradfordians of all kinds thronged in their hundreds on Saturday afternoons, and here was a whole theatrical entertainment in itself of comedians, medicine-men and jugglers. These were in addition to all the pens of livestock for sale, the second-hand clothes stalls and the quick-food counters with their shallow meat pies, their mushy grey-green peas, and their saucers of delicious sea-food.

The comedians were the hoarse-voiced salesmen of everything from cheap underpants to kitchen utensils, and they all had a patter-routine that could keep you in stitches. 'I'm not here for the money,' an expert marketeer called 'Mickey' used to declare, 'Oh, no, I'm here for the overdraft! And it keeps me off the streets. Do unto others as you would unto yourself ... and I'm going to do you proper.'

The 'Quack Market' c.1950.
Photo: Bradford Libraries and Information Service

The medicine-men sold bottles of miracle-working tonics, ointments, strong-smelling creams for every kind of spot or abrasion, corn-scrapers, common cold remedies that were 'infallible' – and anything else they could stir up in their baths and basins at home and cram into the right-sized bottles and phials for their Saturday disposal. People believed implicitly in the efficacy of these nostrums, and went back time and again to pay good money over for the same old rubbish. One soft-spoken confidence-trickster used to claim he could remove cataracts on the eye by the use of his tongue. With his poor victim clamped to a decaying stool he would go to work with a will, licking away industriously at the bare eyeball amid 'ooh's' and 'aah's' from the crowd, until he straightened triumphantly to declare that the offending membrane had gone for good. He would swallow hard, smile a saint's smile and then extend his arms for the plaudits of the crowd. His 'patient' meanwhile seemed clear-eyed and certainly much relieved; and I suppose the sight must have been improved, if only temporarily, by the removal from his eye of some of Bradford's grit and grime. This major operation earned the smooth old gent half a crown a time, and he always made sure the money was paid over in advance.

The jugglers, self-trained, dealt in household crockery. I have seen a man lay six dinner-plates on his outstretched arm, one overlapping the next, and flick them over and about from arm to arm and back again, as easily as a conjuror manipulates a pack of playing-cards. Glasses and cups were tumbled in the air and caught again with amazing dexterity. Uncased, saw-toothed bread-knives were tossed, rotating, from salesman to assistant, and returned with the swiftness of lightweight indian clubs. I never saw any item of crockery broken, nor did I ever witness any blood drawn by the flashing, whirling blades. Jugglers too, of a sort, were the oilcloth-sellers. They worked for a major floor-covering firm called Sharp's, and could unroll a length of lino and flick it back into place with the speed of light, before any marvelling onlooker could spot any fault or irregularity.

One of my favourite characters, and he always drew the crowds, was Young Samson. He was a swarthy young chap, olive-skinned and wild of eye, who always wore a leotard of imitation tiger-skin. His speciality was the bending of six-inch nails, always demonstrated with a good deal of sweat and exertion, to prove the value of the tonics and body-building equipment he sold. Grasping each end of the nail firmly in a dirty cloth 'to protact against the eentense 'eat' (he was some sort of foreigner, Spanish I suspect) he would then go to it with a vengeance, grunting and perspiring until he had formed it into a perfect U. 'There – olé!' He would toss it high in the air, catch it expertly without moving from the spot, and then pass it round for examination, preening and flexing his bulging muscles.

The story goes that he met his match in Norman from White Abbey, a noted Bradford 'knocker' who toured the markets every week, not to buy anything (for that was the job of his unfortunate wife) but to stand with a sarcastic grin on his gaunt features and complain and heckle whenever and wherever he could find the opportunity.

'That's a foreign nail,' this individual laid down one Saturday, after watching the Spaniard's free exhibition. 'Give it here.' And, when it was passed into his hands, 'There y'are, you see. Look at that head – it's as flat as a pancake. If that were a British nail it 'ud be serrated on top – *serrated*!' And with that, the nail was flung back in disgust at the fuming foreigner. Young Samson tried to remonstrate with him, but Norman was already stumping off towards Pie Tom's for a plate of nourishment, and he had to be content with shaking his fist and calling down Spanish curses on the departing figure.

The following week he was in the middle of his act when Norman appeared again, leaning on the wooden frame of the stall and sneering openly at his antics.

'Course he can bend it – 'cos it's all a swizz. Foreign nails, you see!'

Young Samson made his U-shape, tossed it in the air, caught it unerringly and then advanced on his denigrator, holding out the nail with its head almost on the heckler's nose. 'Look – see!' he bellowed, the muscles transforming themselves into iron bands on his powerful forearms, 'Hexamine the 'ead. Surrated – SURRATED.'

Norman was completely unmoved. He peered clinically at the top of the nail through his steel-rimmed glasses, and then played his master-stroke:

'Serrated, aye. Serrated, right enough. Must be a *reject*.'

That was my Bradford, too.

Sunday was our day for the parks, and in particular Lister Park, with its long, macadamed promenade round and about the bandstand, where brass and silver bands gave wonderful concerts in the afternoons of light orchestral classics. I heard my first Gilbert and Sullivan there, and there I grew to loathe, because of its endless repetition, the overture to *William Tell*. Ketelbey was another good old standby, and Tom once suggested they should bundle all his works together and call the opus *Bells Across A Persian Monastery Market Garden*.

On Sunday nights we went to the Rhythm Club, if we could afford it. Cinemas were not allowed to open on the Sabbath and this was the only form of live entertainment available. Before attaining the splendours of the Alhambra it was housed in the Mechanics' Institute, where Dad had gone to join up in the far-off days of September 1914. The Rhythm Club was everything that its name implies and went down well with adolescent Bradford, many of whom would solemnly vow soon to buy a trumpet or saxophone, and then go meekly back home to their piano-lessons or their scrapings on the violin. After our gyrating session at the Club we would go on to the latest craze of Bradford's youth, Farmer Giles's Milk Bar, down on Tyrrel Street. Farmer Giles – and I never saw him personally, though his image always beamed at us from the plate-glass window – sold bowls of thick tomato soup and (an innovation from across the water) milk-shakes of every kind of succulent fruit flavour. The mixture of these two was quite horrendous, and we delighted in it.

If coppers were scarce and Jim Kelly wasn't with us to boost our resources, Tom and I would walk up through Bradford

Lister Park c.1914. *Photo: Bradford Libraries and Information Service*

Moor and pass the old tram-sheds in Thornbury, to visit the Monkey Run. Here, on a stretch of pavement no more than a quarter of a mile long and strictly on only one side of Old Leeds Road (the left side going towards that city, if you should be interested), scores of likely lads and lasses would parade solemnly up and down in pairs and small groups, each unit always being composed of the same gender. The little flagged promenade was regularly thronged. The lads would eye the lasses and make suggestive remarks; and the lasses would titter and pretend to be shocked, as they moved on and away. 'Cheeky monkeys!' But here and there, male and female would sometimes 'click'; and then the couples would consist of one male and one female as Nature intended from the beginning of time. These pairings would move off together to find dark little hidey-holes where they could get to know each other better.

This was where I first met Pat Harker, who was slim, soft-voiced and a couple of years my senior. Pat had something of a Mediterranean look about her, with her long, straight, dark

161

and glistening hair and her high cheek-bones set above a generous, moist and always crimson mouth. She wore a scent called *Evening in Paris*, and it quite swept me off my feet. As I deserted Tom, wishing him luck, we paired off; and she and I crept up Rushton Road to pet and fondle in a dark corner near a garage. She let me stroke her well-developed breasts, and taught me how to give her what she called 'a french kiss'. (I was learning that the French have a lot to answer for, in matters culinary and sexual.) But when she suggested a visit to a local pub I had to disappoint her. I hadn't the money for drinks, otherwise Tom and I would have been down at the Rhythm Club; and anyway, pubs were forbidden territory for me. Pat did not seem too put out and for a while nestled in even closer, so that several more french kisses were soon exchanged. Then she suddenly shook her hair back and said 'Hey love, what's the time?'

'About nine o'clock,' I told her, guessing, because I had no watch.

'Oh God,' she tinkled. 'I've got a date and I'm half an hour late!' And off she went on her clicking high heels, without further explanation or apology. I had thought that perhaps with her evident fondness for close physical contact it might turn out to be quite a night for me. I was wrong, again. What I did not know was that this was only the first of several encounters with the experienced Patricia, and that she had more to teach me than the simple technique of the french kiss.

I had to be very careful in those days of my dealings with the opposite sex for, after the trouble with Albert when he was sixteen, my parents were determined that I should not succumb to feminine wiles at too early an age. My father especially was resolved that 'messin' about wi' lasses' should not be allowed to interfere in any way with my school work. But the call of the flesh is a hard one to deny, especially when you're that age; so I had my private passions but kept very quiet about them. If ever I received any mail my letters were opened and read long before they reached my hands, so I joined the Y.M.C.A., purely in order to have any poor little love-missives addressed to me there to await collection.

162

Forbidden fruit is always the sweetest, and I sometimes wonder if those parental restrictions, all meant solely for my benefit, did not have a contrary effect to the one intended and actually spur me on in my adolescent – but after all perfectly natural – indiscretions.

At all events, the system worked. I sat the exams that summer and got both my School and Matriculation Certificates. I think my dad was the proudest man in Bradford, but brother Albert ran him a close second.

After the results had been announced, Bill Cox called me across the Main Hall to his cupboard, where he was sorting out new school-caps with the blue cross of Turner's House on them. He was the housemaster of Turner's.

'Congratulations, Leslie. A double distinction in English is quite rare.'

'Thank you, sir.' I still could not believe my good fortune. Albert's invaluable advice about an early start to private revision had worked wonders.

'You won't regret all you've done here – especially my little plays. And you can bank on it, English will be your friend for life.' Mr Cox shook hands with me warmly, and went back to the sorting of his caps.

When we later discussed the matter in the privacy of the Head's study, Charles G. Davies's attitude was somewhat different.

'You've done Very Well.' The extra capital letters were present and correct, as usual. 'Yes, excellently – considering all that acting Hanky-Panky. Will you be going on to Higher School Cert. and – Possibly – to University?'

'No, sir,' I told him frankly.

The black eyebrows came together in a frosty frown. 'Whyever not?'

Didn't the fellow have any vague idea? After all, he'd known me five long years.

'We can't afford it, sir. Not people like us.'

'You're a Fool,' he said. And that ended our brief discussion on career possibilities.

On the last day of term I cleared my desk out in Room Ten, packed a few personal belongings (including my Platignum pen) into the leather satchel I had inherited from Albert, and said goodbye to Hanson High School with a heavy heart.

That very night I made enquiries about joining the Old Hansonians' Dramatic Society.

Chapter Ten

❖

A Living to Earn

At the age of eleven, after having watched my father's misery and humiliation when he was drawing the dole, I had vowed never to enter a Labour Exchange again. I was determined on this and, either from being born under a lucky star or through sheer pig-headedness, I have been able to stick to it throughout my working life. So one place I never visited in my search for work was 'The Labour'; instead I wrote a lot of painstaking letters, in the first few weeks after leaving school.

> *SMART LAD wanted for clerical duties and laboratory work. Good prospects. Box No ...*

Soon after this appeared and I replied to it, I was summoned to a firm called Sternol Limited, that had its premises at the bottom of Trafalgar Street off Manningham Lane, near the L.M.S. railway line. There I was interviewed by a Mr Wood, who was looking for someone to discharge the dual responsibilities of junior clerk and laboratory assistant; and out of a dozen or so eager applicants, I was the one who got the job.

Sternol was a London-based oil-firm, manufacturing and supplying motor oils and industrial lubricants of all kinds to northern trades. They had branches in Bradford and Glasgow, and their local premises consisted of a long, low and almost derelict office-building, a makeshift laboratory across the loading-yard, a smaller yard for the solid fuel boiler, and a large old warehouse converted into a vast blending-room on its ground floor and an extensive storage area on the floor above. Mr Wood, who had the joint function of manager and sales representative, presided over a staff of three. First came Jacko the foreman, a Tynesider, whose job it was to supervise deliveries of bulk supplies, organise the blending of crude oils and greases into authentic Sternol products, and ensure their safe despatch by road or rail to customers up and down the land. Sam was his assistant, who carried out his orders in the blending-room and massed the drums and tanks ready for when the haulage-men came to call in the afternoons. Last in line came the laboratory assistant, junior clerk and general messabout – me.

I sat at my desk in the office, which had bare brick walls, a timber floor and an open coal fire. This was kindled in the oncoming winter by the use of discarded bungs from huge, wooden oil-barrels. Their combustion was instantaneous but the resulting stench was awful, and it lingered in the place for hours because the windows were always tightly shut. At the desk facing me sat Mr Wood, if in attendance, and Jacko (the real supremo) on the frequent occasions when the manager was out in his Singer saloon, drumming up business. Set against the wall behind me was a small, trestle table on which rested a ramshackle office typewriter of a much earlier vintage than my second-hand portable at home. In the table's eternally-jamming drawer reposed the Stamp and Petty Cash Book, which was part of my limited responsibility. The tiny desk was my working kingdom.

Orders came in by post each morning, to be vetted by Jacko so that he could set up the day's programme and then passed over to me for entry in the Order Book, in my very neatest handwriting. Then the day's real business would begin. Jacko would make out blending-cards and these were handed on to Sam, who would then concoct the different and required mixtures in the squalid 'works', where great and steaming vats capable of holding hundreds of gallons stood in line to do the blending. In the afternoons there would be tests to be carried out in the dark and mouse-infested 'laboratory'; Jacko taught me how to do this and very soon handed over to me the whole

166

onus of seeing that the ordered blends were of the correct viscosity and present in the required amounts. Meanwhile, Sam would be filling the drums, some of sixty-gallon capacity but most of the tin, five-gallon type. I had to prepare all the labels, and rapidly worked up quite a typing-speed from this; Sam would then attach them to the goods, and we would both see to the loading and despatch arrangements when the lorries and railway-vans called on their rounds. After that there were sample-tins to be filled and parcelled in brown paper before being sealed with scarlet sealing-wax, the day's outgoing mail to be stamped and recorded and, on the way home, the visit to the G.P.O. This massive black building lorded it in Forster Square, in the shadow of the great Cathedral.

I worked at Sternol for just over a year, during which my dreams of becoming an overseas representative and travelling the globe faded and died, as I came to see this was a very small concern compared with the well-known oil giants like B.P. and Castrol. I realised I might well waste years writing in those record-books and typing those accursed labels until I was a very old man, who would probably get sick of it one fine day and chuck himself in the nearby canal. With different luck, I might have been out in the great wide world doing something more productive and of greater interest. But, I kept telling myself firmly, it was a steady job.

And in the beginning these thoughts did not trouble me. The work was far from taxing, the room with its blazing fire was warm and the company was congenial. Mr Wood was a kind and tolerant boss who, although he never discussed the 'good prospects' he had advertised, was unfailingly interested in all my extra-mural activities and even offered to come and see me in a play, if ever I attained such heights in central Bradford.

Jacko the foreman became a great friend of mine. He was ex-Merchant Navy, and had been a ship's engineer before turning his back on the sea to settle down and raise a family. He raised the family but he never did altogether succeed in settling down. Jacko was the greatest Lothario I have ever known, and took great delight in extolling his exploits and conquests to me whenever he was seated majestically at

Mr Wood's desk in that hard-working individual's absence. He was of medium height, stocky, and as poised and hard as a hunting puma. He had straight black hair which was always cut *en brosse*, large, perfect teeth and a gleaming smile that defied you to be downhearted in his company. He told me endless filthy jokes, introduced me to *Eskimo Nell* and *The Bosun's Curse* and encouraged me to change my reading habits and abandon the classics in favour of books like *No Orchids for Miss Blandish* and the then-banned *Lady Chatterley's Lover*. He always had a dirty novel tucked away in his inside-pocket, invariably wore a clean collar and tie, and could be relied on to come up in a flash with a shameful joke or scurrilous rhyme to fit any occasion. His *Ode to Winter* ran:

> *Cold as a frog in an ice-bound pool,*
> *Cold as the end of an Eskimo's tool;*
> *Cold as an icicle – and as glum –*
> *Cold as the fringe round a polar bear's bum;*
> *Cold as charity (and that's bloody chilly)*
> *But not so cold as poor old Billy:*
> *He's dead – sod him!*

Occasionally the final verb was changed for a more usual sexual expletive, but this was a word that, curiously, he normally avoided.

He encouraged me in my limited spare time to extend my sexual experience, and offered to supply me with all the condoms I needed at a cut rate. This was of course a generation before society was to benefit from the ease, convenience and questionable safety of the Pill. When I described to Jacko my miserably inadequate and frustrating attempts to scale the ladder of sex he rocked with laughter and said, 'We'll have to find a lass somewhere to give you lessons.'

Josie was a domestic servant, a breed of unfortunate that my dear departed Grandma Riley had always described as 'dummy-sticks'. She 'lived in' with a respectable family in

Bradford Moor, who ran a small gown-shop and were frequently away at week-ends. She was well-known in the area for being a 'tease', and although not particularly attractive, had a rangy, farm-girl's figure and flaunted a sex appeal that was irresistible to any lad of my impressionable and eager-to-get-on age. You would sometimes meet Josie walking on her own in or near Bradford Moor Park and, even if she did need a certain amount of hustling, she could usually be persuaded up a leafy alleyway or round the back of one of the sheds for what used to be termed 'a spot of slap-and-tickle'. It was thus that I ran across her one crisp Sunday afternoon when, in the middle of our somewhat sweaty embraces, she invited me back to the shop for a cup of tea.

'They're off this week-end, and I have the place to meself.'

The shop was one of a small row that diagonally faced the Barrack Tavern across the junction of Barkerend and Killinghall Roads; and the living-quarters were behind the shop and on the floor above. We went in discreetly at the rear, and Josie soon provided the cuppa that was our superficial reason for being there. It was half-cold and swimming in tea-leaves but that didn't matter to either of us, since it was only an excuse for the real purpose of our visit. We locked ourselves together on the sofa for a while and I tried out the odd french kiss or two, at which I was beginning to feel rather adept. This seemed to arouse in her a much more serious and urgent interest in me and my potentialities.

'Let's go upstairs.'

She showed me her small room, which had only a single bed. 'Look, that's what I have to put up with – can't swing a cat, can you? We'll go in their room. That's double – and I've got to change the sheets tonight, anyroad.'

The significance of this remark momentarily escaped me, but then I wasn't used to girls who took the initiative; and her fumbling and fondling as we transferred to the best bedroom were a new and pleasurable experience. Josie had no inhibitions whatsoever.

'Get your clothes off and get into bed.'

This was more like it, and I willingly complied. She pulled the curtains together and expertly stripped blankets off the bed, so that we should have only a covering sheet for our little escapade. Then she started to undo her blouse, bringing more of her generously freckled bosom into view.

'Do you want to help me?'

I shook my head. I was dumb with excited disbelief at what was happening to me in what seemed, at that moment, the most palatial and promising bed-chamber in the whole of the West Riding.

Slowly she undressed down to mauve camiknicks, and then: 'Shut your eyes a minute.' I did so, and rolled over on my back, wondering how I should cope with this longed-for but somewhat dreaded fulfilment, now the great chance was here. I felt the sheets part and she slid in beside me, completely nude.

A fugitive impression of Blackpool and a slim young figure in a sap-green bathing-suit crossed my mind. But it was gone in a flash, to be replaced by one of the most unfortunate considerations that could have come to me in such a promising context. What on earth would happen if I made the girl *pregnant*? My blood ran cold and, with her eager fingers roaming round my thighs, I suddenly lost my nerve and my capacity.

'Come on, then!' She dragged me in close to her, and put one leg over mine. I had visions of having to tell my dad I had got a girl 'in trouble' ... and every bit of desire drained out of me. 'What's the matter with you?'

'I don't know,' I mumbled miserably. 'I can't seem – I mean –'

'I'll help you.' She smiled wickedly, and her agile fingers did their best, for r̈inutes; but it was all to no avail. 'What's up, love?'

'I'm sorry.' My voice came out a whisper of shame. 'I just can't.' It was pitifully obvious even to the meanest intelligence that I was not going to be able to rise to the occasion. 'Sorry, Josie.'

After a few more futile attempts to spur me back into manhood, she gave up the struggle.

'You're just like all the others.' That hurt – but it made no difference to my problem. 'Let's have a cigarette,' she said, with half a sigh.

Without ceremony and certainly without self-consciousness, she threw back the sheet, pulled herself up still naked as the day she was born, sat on the side of the bed and lit up two Capstan Full Strength.

We smoked in silence. Then, in a flurry of embarrassment, I yanked my clothes on and left her.

'Thanks for the tea – '

'Huh!'

'Ta-ra, Josie; I'll be seeing you.'

'You won't, you know.'

And I didn't.

I had been taught to smoke a year earlier by a neighbour's lad of nine, who was a confirmed addict. I am not proud of it, but I have been a cigarette-smoker ever since. In those days there was nothing wrong with smoking: indeed, if you were well into your teens and you didn't smoke, there was probably something wrong with you. Grandad Riley had his pipe. My father smoked Woodbines, and my elder brother Players. Soon I was being allowed to have a cigarette in the house and this made me feel, without any justification, one of the men in the family.

For the first few years my smoking was very moderate, for I had more important things to do with my money. (I was now being allowed three-and-sixpence out of my weekly wage of twenty-five shillings.) One of these was a luxury I had long looked forward to, a permanent booking in the rear stalls of the Prince's Theatre every Monday night. Arthur Brough's Company changed its plays weekly and operated on a twice-nightly basis, with three performances on Wednesdays and Saturdays. The management offered two seats for the price of one on Mondays, which got the week's attraction off to a good start, and provided plenty of free word-of-mouth publicity whenever the show was a good one. More often than not, it was very good indeed. This concession enabled Tom Pullen and me to have good seats in the pit stalls for the second house every Monday for ninepence each; I have never had such good value for money.

The fare was mostly popular thrillers and comedies. In later years, when I started to make a profit out of writing, these were the models that I tried to emulate, for I have always been a great believer in the theatre of entertainment. My year as a steadfast supporter of the Arthur Brough Players introduced me to many perennial repertory favourites such as *Black Coffee*, *Alibi*, *Distinguished Gathering*, *The Thirteenth Chair*, *The Passing of the Third Floor Back*; and, on the comedy side, *Alf's Button*, *The Magic Cupboard* and (a very early Philip King) *Without the Prince*. But there were plays of a more sober nature too, to educate as well as divert, of which I remember with acute pleasure *For Services Rendered*, *Dear Brutus*, *Robert's Wife* and *I Have Been Here Before*.

The last of these was one of Priestley's Time plays, and it has recurred uncannily during my theatre life. Arthur Brough's presentation of it was my first acquaintance with a work that has since become an old friend. Part of its promotion was the organisation of a competition through the *Telegraph and Argus* (always a faithful supporter of the straight theatre) for playgoers to write in and describe any 'Time' experience they might have had in their personal lives. At Tom's instigation, I decided to enter for this. Using a little imagination, and more than my fair share of dramatic licence, I pounded out this little anecdote on my Underwood:

Some years ago I went to a local cinema to see a film entitled *Perfect Alibi*. There is nothing extraordinary as a rule in going to the pictures, but in this case my visit was attended by a remarkable premonition. Towards the end of the film, the main character fell from the top of a huge skyscraper and hurtled to the ground, hundreds of feet below. As I watched him fall, I had a terrible feeling as if I, too, were falling ... falling ... falling. However the sensation passed off, and for a time I forgot all about it.

A few weeks later, I set out for a long, country walk. Heights had always held a curious fascination for me and it was therefore not surprising when, on coming across some old disused quarries, I peered from the top of one of them into its sinister depths. And suddenly the awful feeling again came over me. I had, I felt, 'been here before', and I was sure that if I stayed there long, somehow I should fall down the quarry.

I tried to laugh away the feeling, deliberately crushing it and ridiculing myself for entertaining such a childish notion. But, five minutes later, while taking a view with my camera of the countryside, I backed a few yards to sight properly – and it happened!

I fell more than sixty feet down the very same quarry into which I had gazed with such fascination such a short time before. Perhaps it was coincidence – but I have other ideas ...

Please note the careful interplay of fact and fancy in this account; and please try to ignore the clichés and the overdone punctuation. Poor Alfie Lister, my erstwhile companion on the ill-fated quarry expedition! He doesn't even get a mention, for I was trying to keep the cast in my little drama down to a minimum. And if he ever read the article when it came out in the paper, he probably laughed his head off at the idea of my owning a camera at such a tender age and in our very reduced circumstances. Me, who couldn't even afford a decent guider!

Laugh all you like, but I won the competition; and I was presented with a box of chocolates by Arthur Brough himself on the stage of the Prince's Theatre on the Friday night of the *I Have Been Here Before* week. That was the first time I ever stood on a stage with a group of real, live, professional actors and actresses.

It goes without saying that I fell in love with one of Arthur Brough's juveniles. Her name was Diana Johnson. She was a gifted actress and, in my eyes, very beautiful. I wrote to her – a eulogy on her supporting role in *When The Music*

Stopped – and she sent me a picture of herself, autographed in a flowing hand. I noticed from the postmark that she probably lived in Leeds, and hoped she had not considered it strange that her new admirer appeared to have his home at the Y.M.C.A. in Bradford. This was the start of an irregular but prized correspondence, that would eventually lead to a memorable meeting and the most harmless of romances.

But all that lay ahead, and meanwhile I myself had a certain amount of acting to get on with.

The Old Hansonians' Dramatic Society was a respected institution that was living through difficult times in the late thirties, owing to the ever-increasing cost of production and the lack of popular support that greeted most of its annual presentations. Mr Cox, my old English-master, had made the necessary connections for me; and I duly introduced myself to them at a play-reading held at the house of one of their members, again in Bradford Moor.

The play was *Time and the Conways* (once more by Priestley), and my main contribution was to assist our hostess in the making and handing-round of cups of tea, mid-way through the proceedings. I cheerfully accepted this as the lot of a newcomer and listened, rapt, to the established stalwarts of the Society, as they showed their paces effectively and with almost tangible reverence for their Bradford-born author.

At the end of the reading I was allowed to deliver a few test-passages, and on the strength of this was offered an audition for their forthcoming production of Clifford Bax's *The Rose Without a Thorn*. The upshot of it was that I landed the part of Thomas Culpeper in their two-night production at the Cooperative Hall in February 1938, and I still have the programme to prove it. I felt very much a new boy, and my efforts (though mentioned in my old friend the *Telegraph and Argus*) did not meet with the whole-hearted approval of our professional producer, Mr James Hall. I have no doubt now that I overacted grossly and tried to make Tom Culpeper the star of the show. This is a great and common fault in young actors, who gradually learn by experience (the best teacher of all) that the whole must always be greater than the part.

Be that as it may, I was soon made assistant-secretary to the society, an honour that I think owed less to my theatrical gifts than it did to the possession of my own typewriter. The secretary proper was Miss Ivy Tolson, the sister of a former school captain of mine who had now gone off to Loughborough Training College to become a teacher. Ivy was a good amateur actress and a shrewd businesswoman, and my friendship with her was to lead to one of the great turning-points in my life before the year was out.

That summer, Albert married Doris Langley and they moved away from Bradford Moor to live in a bungalow at the top of a high hill called Haworth Road. They were on the far side of Bradford now, in the prettily-named Daisy Hill district, on the windy slopes climbing up to the moors and, distantly, the Brontë Parsonage. I was best man at their wedding. Their little bungalow was new, and incorporated a small bathroom that was the envy of the whole family. Albert decorated the place himself (of course) and covered the bathroom walls in imitation tiles that featured marine plants and fish swimming. Therein, at the age of seventeen, I took the first bath of my life over which I could take all the time I wanted. Albert knew how much this meant to me. His wife Doris was loved by everyone and, as I have said, was the sweetest-natured person I ever met. My only pang of regret at their union lay in the fact that the old Albert I had known from birth now seemed to have gone for good. No more duets of *Shenandoah*, no more brotherly confidences about the most private aspects of our lives, no more constant vigilance over my work and pushful ambitions; now the lap-dog was out of safe-keeping, and would have to develop his own kind of independence in a changing world.

But Albert never really left me. He always kept in touch, through good times and bad. Even now, he is only a telephone-call away.

Brother Albert. *Photo: Author's collection*

At seventeen, my attitude towards the opposite sex was somewhat ambivalent. I cherished dreams of an idyllic romance with someone like Diana Johnson, and wrote long letters to her about the plays I had seen and the books I had read, sprinkled with quotations from my favourite poets, those of the Romantic Revival. She replied to these kindly, but always with a note of hauteur. This was warranted, in my view, because she was a professional actress whereas I was only a struggling amateur. On the other hand, I voraciously sought the pleasures of the flesh in the parks and monkey parades of my native city. It was a rough-and-tumble world I grew up in, and you took your fun where you found it.

The night came when I ran into the sexy Pat Harker again, at Farmer Giles's Milk Bar down in town.

'Who are you with?' I enquired, knowing that she would never be on her own in a place like this.

'That crowd over there. That lad in the corner, see? Ginger hair. He's just bought me a strawberry milk-shake and he's dead jealous.'

'Tomorrow night – any chance?'

'Might be – if you promise to be a good lad.'

Surreptitiously, one hand crept down and touched me between the legs, as she turned and waved with the other towards the anxious pale eyes under the ginger thatch in the far corner. 'It's all right, I'm just coming,' she called over. 'This is me cousin!'

'Let's go for a walk,' I suggested. 'I'll meet you outside Peel Park, half-past seven.'

'I'll see.' And that was all. Off she roamed, back to her passing interest of the evening, her long black hair swinging boldly, thrusting her way through the jostling throng as if she owned the place.

I had suggested Peel Park because I knew she lived somewhere near there, and the next night I was at the massive wrought-iron gates in plenty of time; but when they closed at eight o'clock she had not turned up. I decided to give her another twenty minutes after which, if she still hadn't come, the seductive Pat would be out of my life for good.

She came at ten-past, wearing a cute, blue, polka-dotted suit and a small and cheeky straw hat with a tiny veil. The air round Peel Park Gates was heavy with the scent of *Evening in*

Paris, and she was in the most provocative of moods. We walked for a long time round Undercliffe and finally wound up, due to a spatter of rain, sheltering on the verandah of the pavilion at Undercliffe Tennis Club. Here we spread out the newspaper I had hopefully brought with me for the purpose, and lay down together on the wooden planks, after Pat had carefully removed her hat and jacket.

'Like me perm?'

There was no shrugging-away this time, and no pretence of a date with someone else. Instead she moved sinuously on to her back and: 'Touch me ... Go on, I dare you ... *Touch* me.' And quaking, half with nerves and half with unconcealed desire, touch her I did.

'Come on, Leslie. You know what to do ...' Her hands were instructing me by the minute, and growing more and more insistent. Then my old dread of an unwanted pregnancy came back, to flood my thoughts. But on this occasion my partner for the evening was more than a match for it.

'Come on ... come on!'

'I'd like to.' I was whispering again, though there wasn't a soul about. 'But I haven't – haven't brought anything. You know.'

'I have.'

She fumbled in her handbag. I might have thought of the spread-out sheets of paper to shield us from the damp boards and assist in a few passionate embraces and french kisses, but this woman of the world had come prepared for every contingency.

She fitted the condom carefully; and I made strong, passionate, adult love to a woman for the first time in my life. Sheathed love-making I found a somewhat clumsy and abrasive process but there was no doubt that, at its natural culmination, it was deeply satisfying.

Nowadays when people ask me what I think of Wimbledon, I'm inclined to say, 'I don't play tennis, actually – though I'm very fond of the game.'

Hitler was on the warpath again, and extracts from his hysterical speeches (in which almost every sentence finished in a scream, greeted with thunderous yells of 'Sieg Heil!' by his massed worshippers) were frequently heard in the news bulletins put out by the B.B.C. He had already taken over Austria in the infamous 'Anschluss'. Now Czechoslovakia, under Eduard Beneš, was furious with his demands for the Sudetenland to return to the Aryan fold, and the increasing turmoil in Europe seemed to be moving towards a flashpoint.

I walked home one night after a Dramatic Society committee-meeting with Ivy Tolson, my secretary friend, and had a casual conversation that was to change the whole course of my life. It all began simply enough with: 'How's your Jack doing these days?'

'Oh, he's fine. He loves it at Loughborough, and he's student-teaching in the holidays.'

I was very jealous of my former school-captain. He and his family were by no means well-off, though they lived in a better house than ours, a small 'through' in a neat little avenue in Thornbury. Yet he and several others, no better placed as far as I could tell, had managed to go on from Hanson to universities and teachers' training colleges despite their parents' modest circumstances. These lucky lads would soon be carving out careers for themselves in far better white-collar jobs than the one that was my lot. Why should they be so much more fortunate than the rest of us? And what rich old aunt or meretricious trick of fate had provided what Dad always called 'the wherewithal' for such indulgences?

'Ivy, can I ask you something?'

'If you like.'

'I don't want to be cheeky but – where did the money come from?'

'What money?' she enquired.

'To send him on to be a teacher.' It was important to me to know the answer, and if possible to solve the riddle of how I had been denied a similar chance. 'After all, I didn't do so bad at Hanson,' I added, 'but I never got that far ...'

'Oh, it didn't cost us a penny. Except – well, he's not

bringing anything in of course, but they don't mind that. Our Jack did it all himself, on grants and scholarships. He's gone as an R.S.T., you see.'

This baffled me. 'What's an R.S.T.?'

'Recognised Student-in-Training,' Ivy enlightened me. She went on to explain how if you had your Higher School Certificate, which involved two years of further study after matriculation, you could be assisted by local councils and the State to a place at university or in college. Training fees and accommodation would be largely paid for and the balance could be made up out of grants and loans, if the need were great enough. For this help you were morally bound to complete the course and then go into teaching, hence – 'Recognised Student-in-Training'.

It was a revelation to me, one of the few I have ever been granted. My family had never had, nor had we ever been offered, knowledge of these opportunities by any relevant authority. There had been no informative talks at school on this or any similar subject. Had we been alive to the possibilities, no doubt we could have made our own further enquiries in libraries and at education centres. But we were ordinary, working-class folk who knew little of matters academic, and whose chief concern for a number of years had been the wresting of a clean and honest living from an adverse society.

Full of speculation, I hurried home to talk it over with my dad. He listened carefully to every word I said, and I am sure now that he must have had in mind the way he had been balked of his own educational chance long ago, when he had had to leave school to help support his numerous brothers and sisters; he had sworn a solemn vow then that nothing he could help would ever stand in the way of his own children's advancement.

'Do you think you could do it, lad? Go back and start all over?'

'I'd like the chance.'

'Chance, aye; but I don't know if they'd wear it.' He gave me a dubious look. 'After all, you've been left school a year now, grown up into a man.'

This was a fact, and more of a fact than he realised; my friend Patricia had made sure of that.

'Will you see what you can do, Dad?' I begged him.

'I'll try, lad, do me level best. But I wouldn't hold out much hope.'

He wrote to the smooth, squat overlord at Hanson, Charles G. Davies, stating our case in full. That dignitary granted us a short interview in his study.

It felt at the same time strange and warmly comforting to be climbing the stone staircase again up to the Main Hall. Dad, although he had attended every school concert I had been in and never missed a Speech Day down at Eastbrook if he could help it, had never been inside the actual school buildings before. He was visibly impressed.

'Ee, it's a grand place this, Les – grand. Bit different to Barkerend.'

We paused on the landing, for him to study some framed pictures of the William Cox plays I had appeared in when at school.

'I remember that one. Very good. Clever, that Mr Cox.'

We entered the Hall, turned right, and reached the short corridor that led to the headmaster's room dead on time for our appointment. I tapped on the frosted glass inset to the door.

'Come in!' The timbre of the Head's voice was far from welcoming.

'Can I introduce my father, sir? Dad – Mr Davies.'

The interview was short, and totally unproductive. My father explained how we had gained our new-found knowledge and were in search of help so that we might benefit from it. He made no criticism of Mr Davies or his Staff for not having opened our eyes to the possibilities, and rested his case on the simple request: 'I think he ought to have his chance, Mr Davies. Don't you?'

The headmaster was completely unimpressed. Indeed, he seemed almost disinterested.

'It's unHeard-of,' he intoned. 'Your boy did well while he was Here, but the whole success of scholarship rests on Concentration and Continuity.'

'He can catch up. He knows how to work.'

'Look at him.' Davies's tone was almost withering. As he went on I noticed that his old habit, the excessive use vocally of the upper case, was more pronounced than ever. 'He's been Out in the World for twelve whole Months now. There is nothing of the Student left in him. Sideburns!' He now sounded positively disgusted. 'Whoever heard of a Sixth-former wearing Sideburns? And look at those fingertips – hold them up, boy – Tobacco!' He wagged one of his own spotless and well-manicured fingernails at me. 'You've learned a lot since you left Here, haven't you, lad? And it hasn't all been Beneficial.'

I nodded and shook my head. My future was disappearing fast, and there was nothing I could do about it; you don't argue the toss with God.

'You can't help then, Mr Davies?' My father's tone was distant.

'The whole idea's Impossible. I'm sorry, Mr Sands.'

Dad's jaw set. 'Can't help – or *won't*?'

'I've said I'm sorry. Good morning to you Both. And good luck, Leslie.'

'Thank you – Sir.'

I felt it was high time somebody granted him an extra capital letter, for a change.

We left, my father having made no reply to the valediction.

On the walk back home I was as miserable as sin. Visions of Sternol, the testing of evil-smelling oils and the typing of hated labels were stretching before me into a grey infinity. But being with my dad, I tried to keep my pecker up.

'Never mind, Dad.'

'You *do* mind.'

I couldn't answer. He knew me through and through; and Charlie Davies had just delivered a massive kick in the guts.

'We'll have to make the best of it,' I said.

'Will we?'

'Nowt else we can do, is there?' I always lapsed into our native Bradfordian when we were alone together. Anything else, I felt, was more than pretentious in the presence of this man who had been the same, exactly the same, to anyone he had ever met or known; and would go on being the same, exactly the same, until the day I watched him dying.

'Happen not,' said my dad. 'I'll just have to study it out.'

And study it out he did. After having talks with Mother, Albert and that fount of all wisdom, Grandma Sands, he sat down and wrote another letter. This time it was addressed to 'The Director of Education, Town Hall, Bradford, Yorks.'

'He'll never see us, Dad; not now Davies has blocked it.'

'He'll see us – or I'll break his bloody door down.'

Thomas Boyce (and I don't think he had been knighted at that time though he certainly should have been) received us in his parqueted and polished mahogany office, down at the Town Hall. Dad had taken another day off work, which would of course be deducted from his navvy's pay; and I had been excused for the morning by Mr Wood at Sternol, who was keenly interested and wanted me to succeed in my wild aim. Jacko naturally had laughed at me, the white teeth scintillating, when I had told him of my dilemma. 'Load of rubbish! Besides, you don't want to go courting university girls; it's all brains with them – no body.' And he had raised his forearm until it was stiff and erect, with the fist clenched hard.

Again my father stated our case simply and plainly, but this time to a far more sympathetic audience. Mr Boyce listened intently to our hopes and aspirations. He said very little. His bland and somewhat expressionless face only took on a firm aspect, and it seemed to be a look of some concern, when Dad recounted how we had come up against a solid brick wall in the shape of the Hanson headmaster barely a week before.

'Mr Davies is entitled to his own opinions, of course.' He placed his fingertips together. 'But in the end, the decision does not rest with him.' My father shot me a glance, but said nothing. 'Have you brought the lad's report-book with you?' the Director asked.

We had done this, at Albert's suggestion: 'Take it with you, Dad. It's worth a read, is that.'

My father politely opened it at the first page, and passed it over for scrutiny. Mr Boyce settled down to give it his close attention. Out of its records of nine examinations between 1932 and 1937, I had been top of my form six times, second once, third once and (in the year of my quarry accident) sixth. The Director of Education pored over it unhurriedly, reading not only the general results and percentages but also the individual marks and comments, entered and initialled by an array of masters.

At length he closed it, looked at the name I had written in proud capitals on its brown-paper cover, and then handed it back across the desk.

'T. Leslie Sands. I see.'

I was hanging on his every word. My father leaned forward in his chair.

'Well, sir?' It was the only time I ever heard him call anyone 'sir'.

'I'll have your son back at school within a fortnight.'

It had been a crucial September, not only for me and my personal strivings but also for the entire world. At the end of it, our Premier Neville Chamberlain flew back from Munich with a piece of paper that, according to him, was a pledge of 'Peace for our time.'

It fooled our senses, but not our sensibilities; and that momentous autumn, while the youth of this country hoped for the best, deep in their hearts they feared the worst. We took false comfort, willingly, from Chamberlain's promises. And yet, as Louis MacNeice put it in his *Autumn Journal*, we felt somehow:

> *The heavy panic that cramps the lungs and presses*
> *The collar down the spine.*

Chapter Eleven

❖

Against the Odds

Early one Monday morning that October I went into the kitchen, boiled the electric kettle, and had a good wash-down from head to foot. I then boiled it again, and shaved off the long sideboards that had so offended Charles G. Davies's tender susceptibilities.

I had presupposed that on my return to Hanson I would be put into the form that had been a year behind mine when I had been at school before. After matriculation, there normally lay ahead a further two years of study before you could enter university: the first of these was called the 'Subsidiary' year, which took you to a half-way stage; and at the end of the second you sat for the all-important Higher School Certificate, the 'A Levels' of today. Understandably, with my old form now launched on their H.S.C. year I was expecting on that Monday morning to become a member of the Subsidiary year, and they had started work along with the rest of the school more than a month earlier; but, I consoled myself, I would soon catch up on the missing month's studies.

I had reckoned without the Head.

He saw me in his study for a few minutes, directly before morning assembly.

'You're back with us, then?'

'Yes. What form shall I be in, sir?'

He looked at me with an air of injured surprise, as if my year away had made a complete dolt out of me. 'Your Old form, of course. What did you Expect?'

I goggled at him. 'But they're a year ahead of me. More.'

He was unmoved. 'You wanted to come back here. It's up to you to Catch Up.'

'But sir – '

'No Arguments. Go and see Mr Cox; he's your new Form-master.'

That was a blessing, anyway.

And so I became a sixth-former, with two years' studies to get under my belt in rather less than eight months. I have never worked so hard in all my life. And the men who taught me in those three terms of trial were marvellous and quite unstinting in their efforts to help this bulky, blue-chinned and rather bumptious creature whose reach seemed somewhat longer than his grasp. Charles G. Davies rarely spoke to me, but I was conscious that he watched my progress with a doubting and beady eye.

I used to get up very early and do an hour's work at the old wash-hand-stand, while Bill slumbered on in the double bed we now shared. He was ten by this time and attending Lapage Street Modern School, where he was making admirable progress. Hanson school hours were from nine till four-fifteen, and whenever I could I would take sandwiches so that I could pack in an extra hour or so in the deserted form-room while the other sixth-formers were out enjoying their dinner-hour. At four-fifteen I would rush home for tea and then leave the house, Albert's satchel under my arm, for the trek down into Town to the Central Library. This was equipped with a magnificent Reference Section on an upper level. You passed through a long and spotless room, book-lined, with a polished wood-blocked floor and a long, broad counter behind which the Staff presided, to reach the Quiet Room at the far end. This was a good deal smaller, but no less immaculate. It was fitted out with separate cubicles, in each of which stood a table and a hard chair, each cubicle having its own overhead light. If the Quiet Room happened to be packed (and it often was, for scholars of my day took their work very seriously) space could

Interior of the old Reference Library in Darley Street, 1922.
Photo: Bradford Libraries and Information Service

always be found in the large room outside, where stood rows of long, shining, teak tables, benches and chairs.

The Ref. Library, as it was always known, was my regular evening habitat from six p.m. until the Central Library closed its doors. There I would sit, entrenched with my notebooks and texts, catching up on the lost year's work and coping with current homework, revision and preparation. At half-past seven prompt I would leave my books where they lay and go downstairs and outside into the fresh air, to enjoy a short stroll and a cigarette. Then it was back to work until the bell went, when I would walk home with my studies still spinning and weaving through my brain. I could not use my bike on these excursions because there was nowhere in or near the library where it could be parked with safety, and we could not afford the necessary front and rear lights for it anyway. So I walked everywhere, except when a penny could be spared for the tram to take me up the steep ascent of Church Bank and along

Barkerend Road to the first fare-stage. In point of fact, the walking gave me some good and much-needed exercise; and I was getting very little of that, for the time being.

I had been given a modest grant by the civic authorities but this was naturally handed over to my parents, as soon as drawn, to help towards my keep. Somehow, God bless them, they kept me going with a shilling or two of pocket-money now and then; and this usually went on a few cigarettes, table-tennis with the still-faithful Tom, or a single visit to the cinema (in the cheapest seats) on Saturdays. Saturday afternoon and evening were the only times I never grafted, for my dad insisted that I get at least a modicum of relief and recreation. So they were always enjoyed to the full, to be followed by a hard-working Sunday morning and afternoon. On the evening of the Sabbath, I would sink down on the sofa for an hour with the pink *People* newspaper, or listen to carefully selected programmes on the radio.

This was my most celibate year, which is hardly surprising. My only romantic contact, and that a distant one, was by letter with the admired Diana in faraway Leeds. She gave my new way of life her blessing and said that, judging by my letters, I would make a good schoolmaster. She filled her messages to me with details of her theatrical activities with the Court Players at the Leeds Theatre Royal. I sometimes wondered what it must be like to be a proper actor, to be polished and confident and, above all, to be paid in hard cash for doing something you dearly loved.

I can state with hand on heart that at this juncture such a thing was beyond my wildest dreams. To be an actor, it seemed, you had to be not only well-spoken in a B.B.C. sort of way, but also suave and sophisticated; and you had to have a vast and ever-growing wardrobe at your disposal.

I spoke something like correct English by now, but this was kept purely for school and social obligations. It was never aired at home or with Tom and Kelly, lest my nearest and dearest should think I was beginning to put on airs. Also, and even in conversations with my English-master, my voice came out tinged with the tunes and broad vowels of my native heath.

I knew I was completely unschooled in the niceties and conventions of polite society, and was trying to pick these up as I went along. Sophistication was a world away from me and I do not think, after a further half-century, I have ever really come to terms with it. As for my wardrobe, that consisted of two sportscoats and a baggy pair of flannels, a worn blue suit for best, a couple of shirts only, assorted socks, one pair of good brown shoes (I have always been careful of shoes, ever since that evening I played rounders with Gwen Phillips) and some plimsolls or 'pumps' as they were always called up north, carefully preserved from the gym lessons of my previous school career. Diana Johnson was my only connection with the straight theatre, and a lifeline to which I clung with great tenacity.

So there was no cogent reason (as Robert Atkins might have put it) why it should ever occur to me that I might have a future in the professional theatre. Schoolteaching was the limit of my ambition and it seemed unlikely now, thanks to Mr Davies, that I would ever attain that consummation, however devoutly it might be wished. Whatever they might ultimately lead to, I resolved to make the best possible use of my new and heaven-sent opportunities, and to learn through them how to read, write and speak decent English. If I became a schoolmaster, all well and good. If not – well, I'd have my amateur theatricals to console me (nothing was ever going to part me from those) and when this intensive period was over, I'd teach myself to write short stories on my precious typewriter.

In the middle of the year, after a fairly successful Christmas examination in which I came second in the class of nine pupils, I began to suffer severely from sleeplessness; and this has since been a loathed enemy for much of my life. I was driving myself too hard, a fact that was realised for me by my guide and mentor, William Cox.

'Watch out, Leslie – all work and no play, you know the saying. How about a spot of acting, to relieve the tedium? I've written a little piece for this year's concert, and there's a wonderful part in it for you.'

I leaped at the chance and, despite family protestations that no good would come of it, played the lead in the February of that fateful 1939 in his comedy *United Services*. To relieve the strain a little more I led the school dance-band again, later on that evening.

My parents had treated me to a pair of new, silver-grey flannels, and I wore them to and from the two performances at St Clement's. There was a short celebration for the little company after the second and final performance. Dad and Mother had seen the show as usual but, because of the festivities, I was an hour later than they were in getting home. The occasion demanded fish-and-chips.

'We've had ours,' said my dad. 'Nip up and get a cake-and-a-pennorth for yourself.' He gave me sixpence. 'And that'll be threepence-ha'penny change,' he reminded me.

I scooted to the chip-shop half-way up Seaton Street and waited my turn in the short queue. 'And could I have some scraps, please?' But it was late by now, nearly time for them to close; and my supper, when handed over in a folded *Yorkshire Observer*, seemed colder than I would have liked. So I rammed it into my trouser-pocket to keep it as warm and tasty as possible, and hared back down the street. My mother had set the requisite plate, knife and fork, but when I emptied the packet out her gaze was fixed on what I thought were my pristine silver-greys. 'Whatever have you done?' I glanced down, to see that the grease from the fish-and-chips had spread through its wrapping and through the trouser-pocket lining, to leave a nasty, steaming stain all over the worsted flannel.

'Oh, I'll get you another pair,' my dad said, 'Two, if you like. After all, they grow on trees, don't they?'

It would not be long before silver-grey would no longer be a fashionable colour; khaki, navy-serge and air force blue would soon take precedence.

Munich had ceded the Sudetenland to Germany, but Adolf Hitler's appetite remained unsated. In March he took over the rest of Czechoslovakia, and it became clear that Poland would be his next objective. Britain and France now guaranteed

Poland's security against German attack; and in April 1939 measures of conscription were announced by the British Government, under which all young men between carefully defined ages would be required to enrol on a national register for compulsory military service.

'You might have to go for a soldier,' Grandma Sands warned me.

'I hope not, Grandma – I've got too much on me plate. Besides, Hitler might come round.'

'Huh! Pigs might fly.'

In a flaming July I learned I had gained my Higher School Certificate, and there was a high old celebration at Number 12. Some time later Charles G. Davies presided at Speech Day, which was held that year in the Main Hall and not down at Eastbrook as a result of the national emergency. I stood with the Sixth at the distant end of the Hall and heard him declaim:

'This next certificate I present with Particular Pride, since it goes to one of our sixth-formers who, through remarkable Personal Endeavour, managed to complete the two-year course in less than Half of its accustomed Length. Come forward, Tom Leslie Sands!'

'Thank you, Dad and Thomas Boyce,' I said to myself, as amid scattered applause I marched the length of the Main Hall to collect it.

As soon as I knew I had been successful, I wrote to three universities to request a place. In order of preference they were those of Leeds, Bristol and Birmingham. A redbrick university it would have to be, since in my circumstances it would have required a State Scholarship to enter Oxbridge. These were a very rare award in the provinces, and although I had taken the necessary papers I had failed to score one of the Glittering Prizes. To the best of my recollection no State Scholarship went the way of Hanson in that particular year, and so I was not unduly disappointed; I was going to university and that was all that mattered.

Leeds and Bristol accepted me but Birmingham had no place available. I wrote to Leeds a letter of thanks, and requested accommodation during term-time at their men's place of residence, Devonshire Hall. A second letter went to Bristol, thanking them for their offer but explaining I had chosen Leeds because of its proximity; attendance there would obviously save greatly on expenses.

Then off I went to sample the joys of a bell-tent holiday at Stratford again, but this time under my own steam and with three old school-mates for company. It was a glorious summer that year, and we all had a whale of a time.

Apart from our obligatory visits to the Memorial Theatre (where I made my first acquaintance with *Twelfth Night*), we went once more to Shakespeare's birthplace, and were part of a group of sightseers conducted round the historic chambers by the most lugubrious and ingratiating guide I have ever come across. Most of the relics of course, though genuine enough as far as age goes, have little personal connection with Stratford's famous son. The routine went something like this:

On a bed very like this one, William Shakespeare must have been born ... The Bard himself probably looked out of just such a window, though these have been restored, naturally ... From this door, or one resembling it, the great William must have set forth on his walks to the village of Shottery to call on his sweetheart and future wife, Miss Ann Hathaway ... Documents of this nature may have been produced when our great fellow-townsman was unfortunately involved in deer-poaching at Charlecote Park ... William Shakespeare himself loved all things historic – as witness his plays -- and I know he would have joined with me in hoping you have enjoyed your tour of The Birthplace. This way out, please.

The majority of the rubbernecks departed but my pal Gordon Webster remained, strolling round the panelled hall and closely examining various objects, poking into corners, behind chairs and settles, and evidently very much in search of something important. We waited for him, not knowing quite what was going on. The guide was keen to assemble another party, now he had collected the most recent one's tips. He approached my friend with the query 'Lost anything, sir?'

'No, no. Just looking for something ...'

'And what might that be?'

With one of the guide's own ingratiating smiles, Gordon replied innocently: 'I was just wondering where you kept the Manger?'

On the Friday night, with our departure from Stratford looming up next day, Gordon and I took a rowing-boat down the river from Clopton Bridge as far as Holy Trinity Church, where the bones of Shakespeare are fast interred. There was a boatyard in the town then that would let you do this as long as the proprietor was paid in advance, for he was confident you would return the craft to its mooring, safe and sound, before the night was out. (Where could you find trust like that these days?) The chimes of midnight struck as we turned the boat at the church, to avoid the tricky reaches farther downstream. I shall never forget the beauty and the stillness of that glorious midnight on the Avon. Gordon was rowing (for I have never mastered the skill) and I was seated at the tiller. I felt the unalloyed happiness that is youth's prerogative when things are going well for it. I was young, I was healthy and I was soon to go to university. My cup, it seemed, was brimming over.

But it was the calm before the storm. On our last day, when we packed up bag and baggage, took the Midland Red bus to Birmingham and then caught a train for Bradford, men in uniform seemed to be everywhere. Territorials were being called to the colours, and all regular Servicemen were being summoned to their stations. The flashpoint was near at hand.

The date was Saturday 26 August 1939, and the preceding few days had been packed with international developments of the gravest significance. On the Monday of that week, German troops massed on the Polish frontier. On Tuesday, the United Kingdom vowed to stand by its pledge to Poland. On Wednesday, the Nazi-Soviet Pact was signed. On Thursday, Parliament passed the Emergency Powers Defence Act, giving them unlimited scope in the direction of the lives and energies of all the King's subjects. And on Friday, while Gordon and I had been booking our midnight cruise down the river, the Treaty of Alliance had been signed with our Polish allies.

Our nation stood on the brink of war.

Typically, and in accordance with the self-delusion of the time, none of us believed it. Less than a year before we had lived through the agony of Munich, and somehow our way of living had managed to survive. It must do so again, for anything else was unthinkable. In *The People* the fashionable astrologer Edward Lyndoe consoled us with his bold headline: 'There Will Be No War!' In most people's view, Lyndoe was never wrong. This was because his prophecies were usually so ambiguous that he was almost bound to be right, one way or another. But that week's statement seemed unequivocal. So we faithful readers breathed a hefty sigh of relief, and tried to go about our business.

A letter had come from Professor Frank Smith of Leeds University, inviting me to meet him for discussion on Friday 1 September at Devonshire Hall, the men's hostel where he was Warden. I was pressing pants and shining shoes in readiness for the appointment as early as Wednesday evening, by which time the evacuation of schoolchildren had been ordered by the Bradford City Council. So my brother Bill also had an appointment for Friday morning: nine a.m. at Lapage Street School, whence he would be taken with his classmates to an unknown destination. Gloom fell on all the family – except for Grandad Riley, who seemed secretly delighted – and it was decided by my parents that, as Lapage Street was near a bus-stop for Leeds and my own engagement was not until eleven o'clock, I would deliver Bill to his schoolmistress before carrying on to Devonshire Hall to meet the Professor.

Bill was nervous and restless that Thursday night; and, lying in bed next to him, I had little sleep myself. Then we were all up early, his few belongings were packed into a little, brown attaché-case, sandwiches were supplied together with an orange, and he was helped on with his cap and raincoat. A large identity-label was pinned to his chest in accordance with instructions, and just before we left the house his child's gas-mask in its cardboard box was slung about his shoulders.

Hand in hand, my kid brother and I went off up Seaton Street, then turned right to climb the hill of Harewood Street that led up to his school. We spoke little on the journey, though I remember as we passed the end of Curzon Road, Uncle Jack and Aunt Gertie were mentioned; and I found myself wondering if Sands and Grant would soon be off to entertain the troops.

It was drizzling by the time we reached Bill's school, where we threaded our way through a packed playground in search of 'Miss'. We found her, with her band of eleven-year-olds, and I handed my brother and his little clenched fist over into what I hoped would be her safe-keeping. He didn't cry. In fact, I don't remember many of those youngsters shedding tears that September morning, though they were being torn away from their homes at a very tender age, and faced a future that was an imminent and terrifying blank to all of them. Perhaps the majority of them were simply too stunned to express emotion. Long coaches were rolling to a halt in the street outside the playground which, for the forlorn youngsters, had seen many happier hours. I knew I would have to leave, but was finding the leaving impossible.

'He'll be better when you've gone, when it's just – all the travellers – together.' Miss meant it kindly, but I doubted the truth of this.

'Ta-ra then, Les.' It was Bill who had the guts to make the first move.

'Ta-ra, lad.'

Brother Bill.

Photo: Author's collection

We put our arms round each other and I squeezed him roughly, not knowing when, or even if, I should see him again.

'Be a good lad.'

'Right, Les.'

His face was as white as a sheet. I kissed him on the forehead, and walked quickly away.

That morning Warsaw was being bombed by six a.m., and the Nazis were sweeping into Poland.

Professor Smith turned out to be a kindly individual, short and stout, with long, silvery locks and a gentle, almost Dickensian air.

'I think we can fit you in, Mr Sands. Term starts on the second of October and if I were you I'd come over here the night before, so you can settle in.'

'Thank you, sir.' I didn't know if this was the correct form of address for one of his academic rank, but then I was still mainly a schoolboy.

'I understand you do a bit of acting?'

This information had been submitted in advance to the authorities on their questionnaire, as one of my extra-curricular hobbies and interests. There were no Departments of Drama then, and certainly no kind of degree offered in the subject I should dearly have liked to tackle.

'Yes, I love it.'

'My wife runs a little group, here at Devonshire Hall. And of course there's the University Dramatic Society. You'll be looking into that, I suppose?'

'If I've time, sir.'

The argent eyebrows went up a little. 'Keen to get on with the job, eh? Good luck to you.'

It wasn't that, so much as the fact that I had been working against the clock for a long while now, and time-saving had become a habit.

'Thank you for taking me, sir.'

'It isn't the best of times for any of us, but I think you should be happy here.' We shook hands. 'Good morning.'

At sunset that day the Blackout was due to come into operation, and I got home to find Dad and Mother busily fixing up thick and makeshift curtains.

'All right, lad?'

'Yes, Dad. I'm in.'

'I should think so, an' all.'

Mother was too hard at work to comment, and Grandad Riley was staring with open disgust at this latest desecration of his former domain.

'What's t'use of blacking everything out? They'll nivver come here with their bombers. What's there to bomb, i' Bradford?'

But they did, eventually; and he would know all about it.

When Bradfordians read their papers and heard their news bulletins on the Saturday, most of them were now convinced that war would come. Yet we all carried on as normally as we could. Men strode out to football matches and women trudged off to the markets in search of their Sunday dinners. Evacuated children woke up in strange surroundings, and started crying now for their mums and dads. Lovers met and kissed, though many of them must have wondered sadly how much time they had left to be together. The Quack Market was still in operation for those, like Tom Pullen and myself, who were eager for fun and free entertainment. And in the evening the cinemas still functioned, though their frontages were now blacked out and had only a tawdry and apologetic appeal. The following morning the British Government issued an ultimatum to its German counterpart: unless it undertook by eleven a.m. to withdraw all its troops from Poland, a state of war would exist between our two nations. Hitler's bluff had been called at last.

That Sunday morning, I think most of the country decided to forgo its customary lie-in. I know my family did, and we were all up betimes to listen to the radio and await developments. Dad went round to discuss the situation with his mother, as he always did when important things were happening. Albert and Doris were at their own observation-post, over in Daisy Hill. We had no idea where Bill had been taken, but rumour had it (and was subsequently proved right) that he was now near Ingleton, in faraway North Yorkshire. Grandad Riley sat morose and still, smoking the thick black twist in his pipe. My mother busied herself preparing roast beef and Yorkshire pud. That sounds as though we were living the high life by then, and it should be explained that it was always her practice to go down to the Meat Market just before it closed on Saturday night, and wait for the cheap cuts that were almost given away at five minutes to eight before the gates were shut. From there she would return with a joint of beef or lamb sufficient for all of us, and it would have cost only a shilling – sometimes even less. That Sunday it was beef; and I can still smell it sizzling in the oven as I sat there reading, as was my custom on the Sabbath, the *Sunday People*.

My friend Gordon Webster called unexpectedly, to return something of mine he had packed by mistake when we came back – was it only a week before? – from our Stratford holiday. At eleven-fifteen we all heard Chamberlain's broadcast about the ultimatum that had just expired.

'I have to tell you that no such undertaking has been received, and consequently this country is at war with Germany.'

I had only one laugh that Sunday morning, and it came from my perusal of Edward Lyndoe's astrology column in *The People*. The week before, he had ordained 'There Will Be No War'; this Sunday's column was headed: 'A MADMAN AGAINST THE STARS'.

Down at 196 Barkerend Road, watched by Dad and another of her sons, Grandma Sands was making a giant fruit-cake when the news came through. He told us later she received the Prime Minister's declaration in dead silence. Dad and his brother Lennie had both been in khaki twenty-odd years before. They each had sons, and in the circumstances found few words to say.

199

'We just sat there sluffed, Les. You see we couldn't help remembering the last lot, the one they called "the war to end all wars".'

Their mother levered the cake into the oven and slammed its massive door shut.

'That cake,' Grandma Sands announced, 'will not be broken into until the day peace is declared.'

The fruit-cake remained intact in its tin for six long years. Eventually it was disinterred and cut into, for the benefit of the assembled family. It proved to be quite delicious. Unfortunately, Grandma Sands was no longer there to enjoy it.

Chapter Twelve

❖

Cap and Gown

I became a proud undergraduate of the University of Leeds on the misty morning of Monday 2 October, and there and then my courses were decided: English Language and Literature, Medieval History and Philosophy. Two days after I entered university, the National Services (Armed Forces) Act was passed, and all men between the ages of eighteen and forty-one became liable for conscription. That included me. I was relieved that Dad was outside the required limits; and equally so that Albert would not be called up, because as a skilled engineer he was in a reserved occupation.

And so, with most of us under age for the immediate military need, student life began. My fellow-starters were mainly from Yorkshire and Lancashire, though we did have an admixture of southerners in the presence of some evacuated medical students from the Middlesex Hospital, who were a distinctly leavening influence on our dour northern natures. At first I attended all my lectures with avidity, and Albert's satchel was always tucked beneath my arm to hold my books and bring me luck.

The acquiring of textbooks was something of a problem, for up to this point I had been accustomed to having all such things provided by the local Education Committee; but here at university you were on your own. This meant that within reason you were your own boss, and in charge of how many lectures and tutorials you would actually attend and how much free time you would devote to private study. That was a euphoric state that many a sixth-former had long looked forward to. But this new freedom carried with it, as all freedoms must, an accompanying responsibility: apart from your living-accommodation, you must provide for yourself every other essential of the academic life. I had managed to preserve and bring with me a reasonable supply of unused exercise-books from my days at Hanson and at Sternol, I still had my blue-and-silver fountain-pen and have never been short of pencils all my life; but getting hold of the right textbooks was a continuing source of worry. I had been given an increased grant by the Town Hall in Bradford and had also been awarded a small monetary scholarship by the University itself, but these cash resources I had shared with my parents to provide some small recompense for not being at home and bringing in money. The balance, in my newly opened account with Lloyds Bank in Headingley, was woefully inadequate for my needs. So what books I couldn't buy, I went out and stole. Many of the necessary texts I could handle in the well-stocked Brotherton Library, but there were books of reference I needed to have constantly by me, and works I would have to study that would require annotation. This obviously could not be vented on publicly-owned volumes without defacement. Therefore I had to build up my own personal library as best I could. Like most students, I haunted the bookshops of the city centre. My raincoat had large pockets and, when swinging open, it permitted the swift transference of needed books from shelf to pocket. Then I would go, hot-faced and hot-footed, out of the shop and back to Devonshire Hall, sure each time that I would be pursued by the cry of 'Stop, thief!' It never came. In later and more palmy days I sent conscience-money back to the shops concerned, but that did nothing to eradicate a sense of guilt that lingers still.

Devonshire Hall, where we lived and worked in our private hours, was just a short walk across Woodhouse Moor from the university itself. Here scores of males were housed, whose ages ranged from eighteen to twenty-five and whose courses of study were many and varied, covering not only the normal arts and sciences but also specialised subjects such as textiles, medicine and engineering of all kinds. A place in 'Devon' was much sought-after, and those not lucky enough to gain one had to live in digs in mean streets round the university buildings. We at Devon pitied these poor unfortunates and felt they were missing out on something very special; for there was something uniquely invigorating about belonging to a group of youngsters all of similar ages and more or less common interests, developing their minds, characters and personalities in the furtherance of study and the determination to live lusty young lives to the full. There was always something going on in Devon, always an argument to have, always a song to sing. Many were the nights we congregated in the large lounge with its battered leather furniture to hold fiery debates, discuss house business, put on an impromptu cabaret or enjoy long, beery sessions of student airs; I can remember raising the roof there, among a hundred others, with such pet traditionals as *Cats on the Rooftops*, *Little Redwing* and *The Ball at Kerriemuir*.

I had naturally written and told my actress-correspondent Diana Johnson that I was coming to live in Leeds, and hoped that at last we might meet personally. The great day finally came; and, I think for the only time in my two years at Leeds, I pressed my flannels.

The Theatre Royal in Lands Lane had been running seasons of repertory alternating with pantomime for a number of years, and it currently housed a company called Harry Hanson's Famous Court Players. Hanson was one of the historic names in the commercial theatre, who at his wartime peak ran seven or eight companies in towns as far apart as Sheffield in Yorkshire and Bexhill in Sussex. He gave their first chance to dozens of actors and actresses who went on to later eminence in London, in the cinema and on television. He was immensely loyal to his artists and there were some who stayed with him for years and years, making a long career out of being a Famous Court Player.

Though not a permanent member of the company, Diana Johnson was frequently employed by him as a second juvenile or 'ingénue'. I saw in the paper that she was to appear in *Goodness, How Sad!*, a light comedy by Robert Morley. I duly booked a seat for the Wednesday matinée and wrote to her, asking if we could have tea between that and her evening performance. Miss Johnson graciously accepted, writing back, 'How funny to be meeting you in the flesh, after all those charming letters!'

I sat in the stalls that afternoon and had eyes for no-one but her on the stage. By the oddest of coincidences, the part she was playing had the name of Carol Sands; and if you don't believe that, you can look it up in the cast-list.

At the end of the show I went to the front-of-house in Lands Lane and found the stage door. I went through it with a frisson that was not entirely due to Miss Johnson. You see, stage doors of every kind have always given me pure delight – for they enter upon a mystic and magical world that has no equal.

The stage-doorkeeper directed me to a little vestibule with a table, a couple of cane chairs and the back-stage telephone, which was hanging lop-sidedly on the wall. I sat and smoked fitfully, hoping that Miss Johnson would turn out to be a smoker, too. At the end of the lobby was a pair of swing-doors, and I worked out these must lead down to the stage level, and up to the dressing-rooms on high.

Miss Johnson was a very long time in coming. I have since learned that this is no uncommon trait with actresses, who are always bang on cue when required on stage, but usually make a delayed entrance on more personal and social occasions. After what seemed an age, I heard high heels clicking down the steps beyond the swing-doors and knew they must be hers. I stood up, and I think I held my breath. Suddenly the hidden clatter became a confused mixture of a thump, a scraping noise and a feminine cry of distress. She had tripped on the bottom step. The swing-doors flew open and she came careering through, to end in an untidy heap at my feet.

'Let me help you – '

'Thanks.'

I hauled her carefully upright. She dusted herself down and shook her long hair back behind her shoulders. 'Mr Sands?' Her eyes were dancing.

'Yes. How do you do?' The greeting had as much *sang-froid* as I could summon.

'You'll have to excuse me for a few minutes; I must go back upstairs and clean up.'

She disappeared the way she had come; and I sat down and lit another cigarette.

We had tea at the Paramount Cinema, in the Headrow. This was a nineteen-thirties picture-palace *par excellence*. It had a spacious foyer, thickly carpeted, at the end of which were twin sweeping staircases (apparently made of marble) which ascended to a second foyer on the upper floor. Here, entrance was gained to the dress circle and to the long, wide café-restaurant. The approach to this was bedecked with exotic plants and greenery, tanks of brilliantly coloured tropical fish and a collection of brightly feathered birds in large cages. So on your way to the tea and poached eggs, you could remark on a rubber plant (then a rarity in this country), admire a pink-and-white cockatoo and even pass the time of day with a talking macaw, resplendent in scarlet and blue plumage with daffodil-yellow trimmings.

And so we spent the first hour of our acquaintance – and although the tea was passable, the toast was rather charred – putting on airs for each other, and chatting first about *Goodness How Sad!* and her performance, and then about other plays and players. Each of us was pretending to a knowledge and breadth of experience far beyond our tender years. She referred blithely and casually to 'Noel', 'Larry' and 'Emlyn' as though they were old friends, though she had never actually met any of them. I deduced from this that the professional theatre was one great brotherhood of man, in which class distinction had no place (an impression that would soon be corrected when I became a part of it). In response, I self-consciously told her all about my new life at the university, and how I hoped to do a lot of acting and a bit of writing while I was lucky enough to remain there; but these, as I humbly explained, would be of a purely amateur nature.

'Yes. If you'd wanted to be a *real* actor, I'm afraid you should have started earlier.' Miss Johnson, in those salad days, was a great one for putting you in your place.

But she was very lovely. Her shoulder-length hair was a tawny brown, her hazel eyes sparkled and she had a faintly crooked smile that was quite enchanting. Her figure was perfect as far as I could tell, and her legs were slim and shapely. When she walked she took long strides for a woman, and this gave her an almost panther-like tread.

By the time we had filled the teapot up twice with hot water, consumed the last of our iced buns and were on to our second du Maurier (bought specially for the occasion, since this brand of cigarette was named after a famous actor) I was well and truly under her spell.

'I must go now, Leslie.' Again that crooked smile and the frolicking eyes. 'You see, I do like to get in early.'

'Of course.' And then I went out on a limb. 'You called me Leslie; may I call you Diana?'

'Di, if you like. Everybody does.'

I rose to my feet and held her chair for her, smugly congratulating myself that Les Sands knew his manners. The waitress had left the bill near at hand, but this was the first time I had taken a girl into a café and, although I knew all about moving chairs out of the way and helping on with coats, I had no idea that you should leave your payment on the plate for the waitress to attend to it. She would then bring you your change, and you would drop her tip on the plate before you left. All this was undiscovered territory to me; so I swept the piece of paper up grandly, and felt in my wallet for the single ten-shilling note it contained. Diana looked a little baffled as I turned and marched over to the cash-desk in person. She followed. And I am sure she must have had one eyebrow delicately raised, as I paid the bill with as much as I could muster of 'Noel's' insouciance. The cashier rubber-stamped it, fiddled in the cash-register, and held out silver and copper coins.

'That's all right,' I said blithely, 'Keep the change!'

It was there in her palm and she was still staring at me in gratified disbelief, as I escorted Miss Johnson out and away.

Mum wrote and told me that in the first few weeks of the war Dad had gone down to the Mechanics' Institute to volunteer again for the Army. Perhaps some of the old 1914 fervour still coursed through his veins, though I found this hard to credit after all he had been through in World War One. He had been demobbed long ago as a quartermaster-sergeant, and naturally expected his reinstatement to that rank if he joined up again; but for some reason of their own, the recruiting authorities refused him this. I think in doing so they made a big mistake, for Dad promptly withdrew his offer and went off to join a Government Training Scheme that was destined to make a fully qualified engineer of him. I suppose their attitude had something to do with the fact that we were now living through the Phoney War. They may have thought that at forty-four his age was against him; later on, they would not be so selective. Dad shrugged his shoulders, settled down to learn something new, and continued to read his newspaper very carefully.

Little military activity was being reported for the time, however, and what actual hostilities were taking place appeared to be mainly on the high seas. As a result, civilian life had returned to some semblance of the norm. We all carried our gas-masks as we were required to do by law, but the air-raid sirens seldom sounded at this stage.

Spring came, and went. Diana and I were now meeting fairly regularly, to visit cinemas and go on short outings to places of local note like Kirkstall Abbey and the museum at Temple Newsam. We had many good excursions, and enjoyed a lot of animated and affected conversation. But there was rarely any physical contact between us; the old Adam might have been in attendance, but he was kept under strict control. I could put a tentative arm round her in the Tower Cinema or the favoured Tatler in City Square – and was occasionally granted a chaste, goodnight kiss when I walked her back to the bus station – but that was the absolute limit of my sexual conquest. She was on a pedestal, and quite beyond my reach. This did not stop me from writing frequent poems to her, and some of them were published in our university magazine, *The Gryphon*:

> *Thank you for nights of dark closeness*
> *in cinemas, and a mutual interest*
> *in shadowed and impossible lives;*
> *thank you for walks in sunlit countryside*
> *where the songs of birds echoed*
> *the madrigal in my heart;*
> *for teas in city cafés,*
> *and waitresses who smiled and looked knowingly*
> *when there was nothing at all to know.*
>
> *Thank you for talks of dreams, and things*
> *we cannot understand;*
> *for your smile, your eyes, your brow*
> *that lifts so easily*
> *at a chance remark.*
> *Thank you for reading to me in the half-light*
> *and for pauses when I knew not what to say,*
> *and only gazed at you.*
>
> *And thank you for our first kiss*
> *in a moonglow hush that mourned the siren's wail,*
> *and made me think of golden tints on autumn rivers.*
>
> *Thank you for memories, and for hopes*
> *of times to come;*
> *for happiness – and for inspiration –*

And that's enough of that. *Moonglow hush*, indeed! It goes to show you though, what a case I had of Miss Diana Johnson.

While I was enjoying myself at a redbrick university in the North of England, attending my beloved lectures, worshipping the goddess Diana from afar and composing doggerel verse, the German advances on the continent of Europe continued relentlessly. On 10 May Holland and Belgium were invaded, and that same evening Chamberlain resigned as our Prime Minister. Winston Churchill was called in to lead the nation, and the Phoney War was over. The very next day, Anthony Eden announced the formation of the Local Defence Volunteers, and my father was one of the first in Bradford to join. He wore his emergency armband and forage-cap with pride, as along with countless others up and down the land, he drilled with a wooden rifle and awaited the issue of his regulation battledress.

The German army swept on, through the Low Countries and into France. The end of June brought the seeming miracle of Dunkirk. Britain was on her own now, and preparations to resist her invasion became little short of feverish. The Forces trained and drilled night and day. Politicians plotted and planned, and officers of the Senior Staff crossed their fingers and wished for luck. Nationwide, the names of towns were obliterated from signposts, milestones, railway stations and even shop-fronts, to foil the plans of the expected parachutists; ditches were dug in criss-cross fashion over fields and golf-courses, and poles were planted there to deter gliders from landing. And the L.D.V. became the Home Guard who, insufficiently equipped as they were, would act as a trip-wire in the event of invasion, whenever and wherever it should come, to spark off the initial resistance.

Dad got his khaki battledress at last. He had his photo taken in it, and sent me a copy.

That year, most of us did badly in our exams; and considering how unimportant our studies seemed in the face of all these shattering events, perhaps that is hardly surprising. The long summer vacation came, and I had to find a way of keeping myself over the three months or so before my second year would begin. I visited Sternol Limited on the off-chance, to find that my replacement, hired less than a year before, was due to go into hospital for an operation: I could therefore have my old job back, starting almost immediately and at an increased salary of thirty shillings a week.

So there we were, Jacko and I, facing each other again across our old familiar desks and talking endlessly over our mugs of coffee and twopenny bars of chocolate, while the Battle of Britain raged in Southern England, and, in September, war came to London's doorstep in the form of the Blitz.

I had told him all about my registration for military service and how, when asked to express a preference, I had opted for the R.A.F. I had also tried to join the University Air Squadron, but had been rejected for flying because the sight in my left eye was defective; so it looked as though it would be the ground-staff for me.

'Never mind,' said Jacko, 'You'll do all right in air force blue. The birds all fall for the Brylcreem Boys.'

'Thanks a lot,' I answered. 'And when are you going to volunteer for the Merchant Navy?'

He shook his head violently and pursed his lips, the black eyes twinkling above the short moustache.

'U-Boats,' he said, succinctly. Then he rapidly changed the subject.

My second year at Leeds began, and I worked hard to improve on my summer results in the exams at Christmas. This time, these were satisfactory. In the Yuletide season I got myself a job with the Ministry of Agriculture and Fisheries, filling in endless forms dealing with the problems of supply and demand and the rationing of essential animal foodstuffs. This was a far cry from my term-time essays on the classics of English Literature, and my continuing struggle to master the intricacies of Anglo-Saxon. I slept in the Union building three nights a week, on immediate call as a fire-watcher. But the spring of 1941 brought an easing of the bombing and the emphasis now switched to the Battle of the Atlantic and military operations in the Middle East.

Jacko, as far as I had heard, had still not returned to his beloved Merchant Navy.

The urge to act and write came upon me again, and in March I collaborated with Jimmy Williams, a History student from Westmoreland, in my first attempt at an original play. *Midnight News* was a one-acter, and I directed it for the Devonshire Hall Dramatic Society. It shared the bill with Bernard Shaw's *Passion, Poison and Petrifaction*. Our play may have been deficient in passion and there was no poison in it but – judging by the audience's response – it had loads of petrifaction.

April brought with it a greater challenge. The U.D.S. were set to present *Coriolanus*, produced by a senior tutor of mine called Kenneth Muir, a poet, critic and much respected lecturer. I auditioned for the casting committee and to my delight was given the leading part.

Rehearsals were a joy, for Kenneth Muir was full of devotion to his text and had many original ideas for its interpretation. This was to be Shakespeare in modern dress, and the two opposing factions would not represent the battles of Ancient Rome but would reflect, with surprising aptitude, the European conflict as we then knew it. To this end, the Romans were to be modern Fascists, with Coriolanus and his cohorts in uniforms almost as dazzling as those of Il Duce himself; and the Volscians, led by Tullus Aufidius, would be in British khaki. Rudolf Hess, Hitler's successor-designate after Goering, had recently flown alone to Scotland to try and arrange a negotiated peace settlement with Britain. In Muir's production, when Caius Martius Coriolanus defected to the Volscians he came on-stage to the Aufidius camp unshackling the harness of a parachute, and throwing the straps and crumpled silk back into the wings behind him. Muir's whole concept was bejewelled with such parallels.

The first night was a triumph for him. When the curtain fell, having played my first Shakespearean part, I was in ecstasies.

'Coriolanus' in rehearsal at Leeds University in April 1941.

Photo: Author's collection

Diana soon brought me down to earth. 'I think you'll do much better as a writer than as an actor,' she told me. 'I'd hang on to that typewriter if I were you.'

After the show I was invited by some fellow-thespians (evacuated Middlesex Hospital students) to go back to their digs for celebratory drinks and a snack-supper of savoury sausages from the chip-shop in Headingley. Those bangers, which contained not one shred of meat, were a wartime delicacy that fortunately did not survive the peace. The lads were from the sophisticated South, and I could not match their eager capacity for vodka. By midnight I was well and truly blotto – and must have become rather boisterous, for I vaguely remember regaling them with some of my father's comic songs at the top of my loud singing voice. They were a first-rate audience and seemed to find these northern curios most diverting, demanding 'More – more – more!' with much loud laughter and stamping of feet. Suddenly the door of the bed-sitter was flung open and the figure of an irate landlady (the first I ever met but not the last) stood there in curlers and tattered dressing-gown.

'Get that lunatic out of here – and get him out *now!*'

I stood up, trying to muster as much dignity as I could, but my legs would not support me. I was assisted out of the lodgings with some haste and then almost frog-marched up the hill to Devonshire Hall. Here of course it was well after hours. Quiet and surreptitious entry had to be effected, to escape the notice of the bowler-hatted custodian in the gate-house. I have a misty memory of being bundled over a high stone wall, tearing my precious flannels on one of the metal spikes on top, and then flopping slap in the middle of one of the Warden's prize flower-beds. I must have crawled on hands and knees back to my room which (fortunately for me) was now a single on the ground-floor of D Block; and I somehow hauled myself into bed, still fully dressed.

I woke up the next day with one of the worst hangovers in human history. I was dreading the second and final performance, especially since my parents were coming over from Bradford to see me in all my classical glory. I went to my required lectures but took hardly a single note. The thought of food was anathema, and I got through the day on large draughts of unsweetened tea and a few miserable slices of toast which I made for myself, using the radiant bar of my electric fire in D.1. There was no butter. The evening came, and I went down to the Riley-Smith Hall in fear and trepidation, thoroughly ashamed of myself and vowing to give vodka the widest of berths in the future. I did not deserve my place at university and, worse, felt I was about to let Shakespeare and Kenneth Muir down badly.

I stepped on the stage in my splendid white tunic with the epaulettes, my black trousers with the braided stripe and my peaked cap, which was built up in the front to the highest possible point in emulation of the Nazi-Fascist headgear. My stomach was in grave disorder and my spirits were at rock bottom.

> 'What's the matter, you dissentious rogues,
> That, rubbing the poor itch of your opinion,
> Make yourselves scabs?'

Then, miraculously, Doctor Greasepaint was at my side. It was my first experience of this mysterious force that somehow comes to the aid of the actor in distress. I have witnessed scores of examples of it since: high temperatures that vanished completely during performance; sore throats that suddenly and inexplicably eased; physical injuries or disabilities that somehow took a back seat while the play was on. But I do not recommend the good doctor as a routine cure for hangovers; for that, I think, is taking an unfair advantage of his beneficial powers. Luckily, I have never since hoped for or needed his support in any similar emergency.

The play ended with Coriolanus being machine-gunned to the ground, and of course I revelled in this ultra-dramatic moment. The shots were aimed at my departing back. I registered their 'impact' and then spun myself round sharply, to fall heavily face-downwards on the stage with both arms flat out in front of me. It was all very histrionic.

The previous evening this had been followed by a tense pause of simulated shock and horror on the stage, before the assembled lords cried: 'Hold – hold!' Tonight they had no chance. As I hit the deck with a crash, an anguished female voice cried out from the back of the packed hall: 'Hey! What have they done to my lad?' It was overlapped by an agitated hiss of 'Shut up, Alice! It's only a play.' Once again my mother, who took absolutely everything at its face value, had allowed her maternal instinct to get the better of her.

As I left the stage, I noticed blood dripping from my right hand. When I examined it I found that my extended palm had hit the boards with such force in my 'death-fall' that the skin had split diagonally to a length of about three inches. Luckily, my mother had not spotted this, or she would have been up on that stage in a trice and laying about her with a fearful vengeance.

Afterwards, I had to remind them about my registration, and break the news that my call-up could come at any time.

My dad's face fell. 'They'll let you finish your course though, surely?'

'That's another year, Dad; they might not.' And I explained

that whereas all science students were automatically granted deferment until they had graduated, such a privilege did not extend to students in the arts faculty; their talents, in the official view, were not in such urgent demand in time of war.

He grew indignant. 'They want their brains testing! What are they going to do for teachers after this lot?'

In the event he proved to be right. There was a very serious shortage of fully qualified arts-masters in secondary schools by the beginning of the next decade.

I spent the early summer revising like mad for my Intermediate B.A. exam in June. When the results were published, I learned I had passed with a modicum of credit. Once more, Albert's dictum about early revision had proved its worth.

So there I was now, with the long summer vacation of three months in front of me. I had no money to live on, and the chances of completing my degree course were becoming more and more remote as the War Effort accelerated. In the Yorkshireman's term, I felt stuck fast.

Eric Mitchell was a Middlesex student who had given us a notable Menenius in our recent Shakespearean production, and one day we talked together over a cup of tea in the Union.

'Going home for the long vac?' he asked me.

'No, Eric,' I told him, 'I have to get a job. Can't live on fresh air till October.'

'Know what I'm going to do?'

'What?' I was interested, for I knew he was a man of commonsense.

'Write round to the repertory companies,' he told me. 'See if any of them want summer help. I can sweep a stage up ... and they might even let me do a bit of acting.'

That night I sat down and wrote to Harry Hanson at the Theatre Royal. I asked him straight out to give me an early audition. As far as I was concerned, they could forget the sweeping-up bit.

Hanson's office was at the top of the first flight of stairs beyond the vestibule where I had first encountered Diana. It was the tiniest of dusty rooms, entirely functional, and swamped in playscripts, posters and old theatre bills. He was a small, plump and prosperous-looking man with a penchant for neat toupees, suede shoes and well-tailored suits. On Independence Day in 1941 the toupee was a gingery one and the suit was made of chocolate-brown worsted. We went through a scene from the American play *Smilin' Through* together, with me reading Willie Ainley and Hanson himself reading all the other parts. At the end of it, he leaned back in his swivel-chair and studied me for what seemed like an age. He had bright blue eyes that were somewhat prominent, but there was kindness behind their penetrating stare.

'Your English isn't bad, but you speak with a Yorkshire broad 'a'. You'll have to get rid of that.'

This conveyed nothing. Was it to be 'yes' or 'no'? Or even 'maybe'?

'I'll tell you what I'm going to do.' He reached for another script. This time it was *Bird in Hand*, by John Drinkwater. He opened it at a test-scene. 'Take this home and learn the part of Beverley. Those two pages there. Come and see me Wednesday next, same time. We'll see if you can learn lines properly.'

I went home that Friday evening in a dream. The holidays had started now, and I was back in Seaton Street. My father had his doubts about my course of action.

'I thought you wanted to be a schoolmaster?'

'I wanted an education, Dad. Teaching was the only way. R.S.T. – remember?'

'I remember.' Then, insistently, 'But you *will* take your degree?'

'If they let me.'

'They'd bloody better.'

'There's nothing else'll stop it and that's a promise.'

'All right, lad.' He sounded relieved, but still doubtful. 'I only hope you know what you're doing.'

That week-end I went up into Peel Park to escape the family's questions and my Grandad Riley's disapproving grunts and snorts. Again the summer was a glorious one, and I sprawled out full-length on the grass to devote myself to a study of Cyril Beverley. Within an hour I knew those two pages inside-out; and I knew everybody else's lines, as well as my own. Wednesday seemed an awfully long way away, and I went round in the interim practising inflections and teaching myself how to pronounce words like 'dance', 'prance' and 'advance' with a long 'a', in an imitated southern drawl. I longed for Diana's tuition but did not dare to ask for it, so I relied instead on the B.B.C.'s announcers, listening to them carefully and trying my best to emulate their pace and evenness of delivery. I was going to show Harry Hanson what actors might be made of, come that Wednesday.

On the Tuesday morning a telegram arrived: PLEASE CALL THEATRE TODAY 5 PM TO GIVE AUDITION – HANSON. Something untoward had come about, and the audition had been brought forward by a day.

I was there an hour too early, and walked round and round the block until it was time to go inside. I longed for a cigarette but the bus-fare from Bradford had cleaned me out, and I would have to wait until I got home to borrow a smoke from Dad.

Hanson auditioned me carefully, asking me to repeat various bits and actually going on to produce me in them. Then came the pause and the piercing cobalt gaze once more, as he studied me before coming to his decision.

'Right.'

He explained that one of the juveniles in his Sheffield company had received his calling-up papers out of the blue, and this necessitated a replacement at extremely short notice for an important part in *Do You Remember?* The play was due to open at the Lyceum on the following Monday, and the cast were already in rehearsal. They had 'set' the play (been given positions, moves and grouping) that very morning, and the next day they would be rehearsing Act One without scripts. Did I feel up to the job and could I learn the first act overnight? I assured him that I did and that I could.

'Good luck to you. Here's your copy. Be at the theatre at ten. The producer's name is Alexander Marsh. He'll know it's your first job, but nobody else will. If I were you I'd keep a bit quiet about that.'

'Thank you, Mr Hanson.'

'You haven't asked me about money.'

'It's not important.' (Had I actually heard myself saying that – I, a dyed-in-the-wool Sands?)

'I'll pay you five pounds a week.'

'That's fine.'

I didn't tell him it was wealth unheard of.

I drifted down to Wellington Street in a daze, to wait for my bus back to Bradford. Next to me in the queue was a young lad of eleven or twelve, who leaned back against the dirty glass panel of the shelter as he glanced through some sort of comic paper. As he turned the pages I could not help but notice how fashions were changing in reading-matter for the young. The stories were nearly all told in pictures with captions, most of their plots being conveyed in dialogue-balloons that issued from the characters' mouths. There seemed to be none of those long yarns in very small print, telling of the exploits of people like The Black Sapper, Rex Remington of the Bar 8 and the Wolf of Kabul, such as we used to encounter weekly in rattling good mags like *Rover, Adventure, Skipper, Wizard* and the later *Bullseye* and *Hotspur*. Even our earlier comics, devoured with gusto, had always had real stories in them among the ones that were told in childish pictures. The *Rainbow* had regularly featured plenty of these, and that was one of the reasons I had always coveted it. I suppose I only attained it three or four times in my childhood because it cost tuppence, as against the single penny charged for the regulation black-and-whites.

Now I found myself trying to save up for the *Rainbow* all over again. But this rainbow was somewhat different from those few sheets of paper with the front cover in full colour. This rainbow stretched far above me and, even if I could never reach it, had more vibrancy and iridescence than anything I had ever known. It was the rainbow of the Theatre, and there was just a chance now that in its shimmering beauty it might well span the rest of my life. I wanted desperately to buy it, but did I have the necessary tuppence? This gorgeous arc was not available in coinage of the realm; its purchase could only be measured in terms of talent, determination, chance and stamina. I was dealing in imponderables here, and simply did not know if I had enough in my own purse to cover the cost.

Meanwhile, there were matters of more concrete and immediate finance that had to be considered. As far as actual money was concerned, I had as usual no working capital. Once aboard the double-decker bus, I weighed up my prospects on the ten-mile journey home. There would be rail-fares to pay to and from Sheffield for the rest of the week, during which I would have to find somewhere to stay in that unknown city for the week of the performances. There would be incidental snacks and the odd cups of tea or coffee to settle up for. Harry Hanson had made it clear there would be no rehearsal money and, although some expenses would be paid on the Friday of the rehearsal week, I wouldn't get my salary for another nine or ten days. Meanwhile I had to travel, and I had to feed myself (certainly for that following week) in new and strange surroundings.

And then I saw the way out.

I let the bus over-run my usual stop and got off at the bottom end of Garnett Street. I walked up this forbidden territory of my youth, peeped down Grant Street for old times' sake as I passed it, and turned the corner into Barkerend Road. I was making for Number 196, to carry on a family tradition.

Grandma Sands had the kettle boiling on the hob of course, and tea and ginger biscuits were soon forthcoming as I outlined my predicament to her. She moved slowly these days on account of her age and massive weight, and I noticed her breathing had become wheezy and rather laboured. However she had not lost her habit of whistling little tunes under her breath, something she always did when she was concentrating. I find myself doing the same thing to this day when I have something on my mind, and know then that a bit of her lives on in me. As always, she kept me waiting; but this time not for long.

'How much do you want?'

'I hardly like to tell you, Grandma.'

'Let's put it another way; how much do you *need*?'

You had to be direct with her, there was never any other way. So I came straight out with it: 'Could you lend me three pounds till a week this Friday?'

The steely grey eyes glittered with seeming alarm. 'Three pounds? That's a lot o' money.'

'I can't see me managing on less. I'll pay the usual interest.' I was wishing now that I had been born with my dad's charm and powers of persuasion.

To my surprise, there was no more dilly-dallying. Instead, she lumbered to her feet and crossed to where her large handbag rested on the black chiffonier. Standing there and still half-whistling some unidentifiable catch, she felt inside it and counted out three one-pound notes. She brought them to the table, sat down and placed them between us.

'Thanks, Grandma. I didn't know who else to turn to.'

'They only come here when they want summat.' There wasn't an ounce of sentimentality in the woman.

'How much will the interest be?' I had to ask, for that would have to be taken into account.

'No interest – this time round.'

'You what?' I stared at her in honest amazement.

'You heard me.'

I'd heard all right, but I couldn't believe my ears.

'You *always* charge interest.'

'Not allus.' She looked away from me, and her voice went oddly quiet. 'After all, that's not going on booze, is it?'

'No, none of it.'

'Pick it up then, and get from under me feet.' My grandma looked back at me, and now her voice had its usual cutting edge. 'I thought you had some words to learn?'

I told my mother and dad, when I got back. 'You jammy bugger', he said. 'She allus had a soft spot for you, Grandma Sands.'

I was up till well after midnight, seated at the old wash-hand-stand in the bedroom with my script in front of me; my brother Bill, now happily rescued from evacuation, slumbered on contentedly in the big double bed; and I knew that first act thoroughly before I put the light out.

Lyceum Theatre, Sheffield

Proprietors - - - The Sheffield Lyceum Theatre, Ltd.
Managing Director and Licensee - **JOHN BEAUMONT**
Resident Manager and Treasurer - A. E. HOLLAND

5.30 - TWICE NIGHTLY - 7.45

Week commencing **MONDAY, JULY 14th, 1941**
For Sheffield Court Productions Ltd.

HARRY HANSON presents

The Famous Court Players
in
THE DELIGHTFUL COMEDY

DO YOU REMEMBER?

By EDITH SAVILLE & JOHN CHARLTON
From the Vaudeville Theatre, London W.

WAR TIME **Programme 2ᵈ**

Do You Remember? The author's first professional stage appearance.
(See overleaf also)   *Programme from the author's collection*

The next Monday, after four days of travel and hard slog and a Sunday spent in assembling a presentable costume for the play, I checked in at a Sheffield guest-house and then took my bag and my *Nignog Revue* make-up box (carefully preserved) along to the dress rehearsal at the Lyceum. I shared a dressing-room with Terence Alexander, who is these days a leading actor on stage and television. He coached me on some of the finer points of repertory make-up and the art of underplaying, at which even then he was a pastmaster.

Some telegrams were waiting for me on my dressing-table.

I'VE GOT MY FINGERS CROSSED
DARLING – DI.
BEST WISHES FOR A CHARACTERISTIC
TRIUMPH – COX.
CONGRATULATIONS AND GOOD LUCK –
GAFFER.

At five-thirty prompt on 14 July 1941, the curtain went up at the Sheffield Lyceum on *Do You Remember?* by Edith Saville and John Charlton. Leslie Sands was down in the programme to play Peter Storm. Within minutes, I was on the stage and earning my crust as a professional actor. It was a highly improbable dream come true – and I was already three pounds in the red.

DO YOU REMEMBER?

John Winter	MAURICE PRICE
Cornelia Hepplewhite	CISSIE ASHLEY
Peter Storm	LESLIE SANDS
Horace Fortesque	PETER COLEMAN
Bruce Wolf	TERENCE ALEXANDER
Diana Fellowes	DOROTHY BAIRD
Gladys Brown	DOREEN LAWRENCE
Mark Collerain	ROBERT WOOLLARD
Mrs. Fellowes	BERYL MACHIN
Ethelinda Paske	CHRISTINE S. WILLIAMS
Restaurant Attendant	JAN FOGARTY
A Passenger	LESLIE SANDS

Play produced by ALEXANDER MARSH
Scenery Designed and Executed by
HERBERT GOOD and JACK JACKSON

Chapter Thirteen

❖

Chasing Rainbows

Never mind yer mother, suck yer jaffa –
The second house begins at nine o'clock!

That was an old music-hall snatch my dad often used to bawl out at the top of his voice, when he had had a pint or two.

The second house at the Lyceum that night provided several useful lessons in stagecraft, one of which I have applied ever since.

The play was a sentimental comedy about student life and young love. The scene almost throughout was a studio in Soho, where several semi-bohemian young people indulged in the amorous and almost farcical pranks customary in such theatrical settings. They had the usual ambitions – literary, artistic and musical. I was the playwright, and Terry Alexander was the embryonic musical virtuoso. The whole shebang was what repertory publicists used to call 'a human story of laughter and tears', and provided the kind of harmless fun that was then very popular with family audiences in the provinces.

In Act One, the 'students' somehow managed to acquire a crate of ale for some minor jollification; and it was my job to pour out drinks for the three or four of us on stage. Actors' appetites for left-over 'properties' of an eatable or drinkable nature are voracious. A wise old prop-master had decided shrewdly that two pint bottles of genuine ale per performance would more than meet the script's needs and avoid 'wastage'. He had consequently filled the rest of the pint bottles in the crate with water from the tap. The bottles themselves were of dark brown glass, and therefore the two practical ones were indistinguishable at first sight from their harmless fellows. Regrettably, nobody had taken the trouble to warn the newcomer of this. Luck must have been on my side during the first house, because then nothing went amiss. However in the smoky conviviality of the second, I drew a bottle from the crate, unscrewed the top, said 'What about a spot of this, then?' – or some such nonsense – and proceeded to pour out a generous helping of clear, cold water. The people in front loved it. They always do, if there is an accident in performance and they can grasp immediately what has gone wrong. These mishaps are then often greeted with a quick round of applause, after which seasoned theatregoers are ready to forget the whole thing and settle down again to the matter in hand. I gaped at this travesty of alcohol and, to cover, stammered, 'Beer's not what it used to be.' This got another laugh. Terry Alexander, whose quick wit was always ready in any emergency, followed up with: 'Ah well, there's a war on.' This went down even better – despite the fact that the play was set in peacetime, long ago and far away.

Lesson: always check your personal props before every single performance.

After the somewhat rocky opening night – and none of them could be perfect, when rep artists were doing a different play every week and that twice-nightly into the bargain – the show went well, and received excellent notices.

Harry Hanson himself came to see the first house on Friday evening and sent for me between the shows. I ascended to the manager's office, fearful that I would be told I was not good enough for the job, and was delighted when, on the contrary, he seemed reasonably pleased with me. This time the suit was of dove-grey gabardine and the toupee was in matching silver.

'I have a play called *Smilin' Through* on tour. You read a bit of it for me when you came to Leeds. If you like, you can join the tour on Monday.'

It may seem that I was extraordinarily lucky in my first two engagements; but opportunities like this were cropping up often, as more and more young men received their papers

Acting of course was far from being a reserved occupation, and many of my friends in the business today might never have gained their first chance had it not been for such wartime exigencies.

Smilin' Through had been on the road for a number of weeks and, the usual story, one of the cast had been called up and was required for national service in a week or so's time. He could play Barnsley the following week but would then have to withdraw from the part of Willie Ainley, the character-juvenile haplessly and hopelessly in love with the play's heroine, Kathleen Dungannon. I could join them at Barnsley, rehearse the part that week and open at the Theatre Royal, Hanley, the following Monday.

The bag was packed, the debt to Grandma Sands was paid and I was off on my wanderings again, in the footsteps of (as I saw it) great names like Fred Terry *(The Scarlet Pimpernel)*, Johnston Forbes-Robertson, Henry Ainley and John Martin-Harvey (the greatest Sydney Carton of them all, in *The Only Way)*.

When I got there, I found Barnsley grey and utterly depressing. The theatre was echoey and decrepit and the stage-doorkeeper had no digs-list to offer. I was not required officially until the evening, when I was to watch the show from the front and study Willie Ainley's participation in it, so the afternoon was mine to explore the town and find somewhere to lay my head that night.

I had no experience at all of hunting for digs, and therefore enlisted the help again of my old friend the Y.M.C.A. They did not provide sleeping accommodation, but recommended me to try a Commercial and Temperance Hotel near Barnsley's market. 'Commercial and Temperance' seemed to me to be a contradiction in terms, but I went along there and tried my luck. The manageress, a slim, dark and fetching lady in a tight-fitting black dress, was most sympathetic and left me with a cup of good coffee while she went off to consult her registers. There was a tall, revolving bookcase in the lounge, and I studied its contents while I waited for her. It had the usual rows of thrillers and travel books ... and then I noticed on the bottom shelf a collection of issues of a magazine called *London Life*. I have always loved magazines, so I took one out to sample its contents with my coffee. I found to my surprise that some of the photographs and articles were rather daring (for the time) and this hardly seemed to fit in with the oak panelled walls, sober decorations and Landseer prints in the place, normally frequented presumably by only commercials and temperates. There was a Readers' Letters section that was full of accounts of riotous parties, where fetishists of various kinds had got together to indulge their fancies as group. Rubber and leather figured prominently in many of the contributions. Further submissions to this feature were eagerly invited by the anonymous editor; and God knows what kind of a private life he must have indulged in.

'You like that sort of thing?' The lady in black had silently returned, and was standing there watching me with a faint smile on her face.

'Very interesting.' I shot to my feet and hastily put the magazine back in its place.

'So you're an actor?' She was the first person who had ever addressed me as such. Buoyed up by my single week's experience of professional acting I nodded, rather self-consciously. 'You might say that,' I replied.

'Splendid.' The smile was still there, and now seemed to have become inviting. 'I've got a nice single available on the first floor. Half-board, two pounds for the week. Or I could arrange bed-and-breakfast, if you like?'

'Half-board will be fine.' I didn't really know what it meant.

I inspected the room, found it austerely comfortable, and dumped my bag. As I was leaving, with my script tucked safely under my arm, she said: 'Good luck with the show. Pop in and have a drink when you get back, tell me how it went.'

I thought about explaining that I wasn't acting that evening, only watching, but thought better of it.

'A drink?' I asked her.

'You do drink, don't you? All actors do.'

'Sometimes,' I assured her. 'But only beer.' I had sworn off spirits of any kind after my revel during *Coriolanus* with the Middlesex Hospital undergraduates.

'I've got plenty.' And she moved a step closer.

'But I thought this was a temperance hotel?'

'Not beyond that.' She pointed to a notice that said 'Strictly Private', mounted on a door leading off the lobby. 'See you later. Don't forget.'

Smilin' Through (and I hope its author will forgive me) was a rather trivial piece that came to us from America. It was filmed twice by Hollywood, but despite that distinction now seems to have sunk without trace. In this typically sentimental romantic drama, three generations of complications followed the accidental killing of a Victorian lady by a jealous swain on the day of her wedding. Its two memorable features were a flashback in the second act (a fairly novel device then, in straight drama) and a rendering of the play's eponymous theme-song, done in front of the curtain by a member of the cast between two of the acts. This was sung in our production by a talented actress with a beautiful voice. Her name was Margaret Ramsay. Peggy Ramsay has eschewed acting for a good few years now; but the profession's loss has been authorship's gain, for she is these days one of the best literary agents in London.

Willie Ainley, the character I obviously studied most closely that night, had one appearance in Act One and one in Act Three. He played no part in the 'flashback' act and this, I remember thinking, would give me plenty of time in the dressing-room to get on with my studies. I made a mental note to collect some textbooks from home the following week-end.

I had learned all my lines the day before and so, after fish-and-chips eaten out of a newspaper in Barnsley's market-place, the world was my oyster until rehearsal the following morning; and I returned to my hotel ready for the celebratory drink that had been suggested so charmingly.

The manageress, it transpired, was a young widow who was running the place alone and apparently quite successfully. She gave me two glasses of Bass and we had a long chat about her and then about my new way of earning my keep. Later in the week she proved even more accommodating. Remembering that collection of magazines, I was glad to discover she was not a manic of any kind and her appetites, like my own, were healthy, normal, and in need of satisfaction.

During that glorious summer, while Churchill and Roosevelt were drafting their Atlantic Charter, *Smilin' Through* visited Hanley, Bradford, Lincoln, Keighley, Edinburgh, Minehead, Ilfracombe and Glasgow, before I had to leave it.

The Potteries did not impress me, but I was delighted to tread the boards at the Prince's Theatre in my home town. While there, I went back to Hanson School to see the masters who had given me such loyal encouragement in my new venture.

William Cox, who bestowed some sort of accolade when he invited me to call him 'Bill', was delighted that I was now gathering professional experience, and peppered me with questions about life on the stage and off.

Gaffer was his usual bland and rubicund self. 'You'll meet a lot of fascinating people,' he commented. 'In fact, I rather envy you.' I considered telling him about the hotel manageress in Barnsley, but thought better of it in view of his sexual preferences. 'I suppose so,' I answered instead. 'As a matter of fact, I have already.'

Charles G. Davies was seated on the dais as I passed through the Main Hall on my way out. He was bundled up in his black gown and looked like a well-fed, lordly raven. I crossed over to his desk to pay the necessary homage.

'Enjoying life, are you?'

'Very much indeed, sir.'

'Better than School ... or University?'

'I wouldn't say that,' I told him. 'But it's nice to be paid for doing something you love.'

'My sentiments exactly, about Teaching,' said the Head. 'And you won't forget your Third Year starts in October?'

'I won't forget.'

He lifted his eyes from his papers and favoured me with the basilisk stare of old. He had saved his best capital letters for last.

'So what do we Call you now, then – Aubrey Vere de Vere?' I swear those were his exact words. 'Or have you decided to Stick to the more commonplace Leslie Sands?'

'There's nothing wrong with it as a stage-name, sir. And my father likes it.' I could not resist the dig. But if it registered, he gave no sign. 'I've heard Better,' was his only comment. One solitary sniff of pure disdain, and back he went to his documents.

'Goodbye, sir.' And I meant it, for I never saw Charles G. Davies again.

There can be no doubt that he and I suffered some sort of personality-clash of our time. I don't think I upset his apple-cart very much, but he certainly rocked mine rather unpleasantly. I've met many schoolteachers, before and since, but he badly dented my faith in and my respect for a noble profession. On the other hand, I picked up quite a lot from him about the value of timing, the art of inflection and the strength of stillness. Further than that, he taught me (without meaning to) that the use of capital letters should be mainly reserved for the beginning of sentences and the introduction of proper names. Oh – and I learned about insomnia from him.

As the tour went on, I not only rapidly became used to living the life of a strolling player but also acquired the knack of finding accommodation for myself quickly and at a reasonable cost. I found in Edinburgh the best 'digs' I have ever come across. There, a bonnie Scots landlady with a face like a hatchet and a heart of purest gold gave me my own large bed-sitter with a coal fire, a double bed all to myself, unlimited hot water for baths and full board (four square meals a day), all for two guineas a week. Think of that, you big spenders, next time you lay out

£130 a night at the Savoy for a single room – without breakfast. This angel of providence was Mrs Hedgeland of 35 Castle Terrace, and that name and address will never fade from me.

Talking of landladies, the worst I ever came across happened along the week after, when we played the Queen's Theatre in Minehead. Understandably enough, I have forgotten her name; but I do remember she was of Cockney origin and was one of the meanest people I have ever met. I stayed there with the assistant stage-manager, Richard Butler, and we shared a single room that had somehow had two beds thrust into it. There was no heating of any kind, and hot water was only forthcoming if you fed endless shillings into a contraption that controlled an ancient geyser in the bathroom. The meals were doled out in minuscule portions and the main courses were badly cooked to the point of a trencherman's despair. As for dessert, every single day we had bread-and-butter pudding, and only that. A framed photograph of the tyrant's late lamented husband gazed down at us constantly from the greasy wall of the tiny dining-room. He was dressed in black and had a high, starched collar, a ferocious expression and a very off-putting squint. I do remember his name because it was so constantly repeated in her conversation: it was *My George Albert*. Because our week there had been so terrible, Richard and I planned to do the next leg of the tour travelling in the lorries that would take our scenery, furniture, wardrobe and props over to Ilfracombe after the conclusion of the performances on Saturday. This meant we would not be staying the full seven nights we had booked with the old bat, and we summoned up enough courage to ask her for an appropriate reduction in terms.

'Reduction?' Her face turned to parchment and her voice grew shrill. '*Reduction*?? I never heard the like! You've eaten me out of house and home and now you're asking for a REDUCTION?'

'It's just that we don't get paid all that much –' Richard started, but he got no further.

'You'll get no reduction here! Oh, My George Albert would have told you a thing or two!'

230

'If you want the honest truth –' and my voice was just as shaky as Richard's had been, 'I don't think we've had value for money anyway.'

'Oo, young 'uns nowadays! You don't know you're born. If only you'd been through what I have –'

'The beds are awful.' My friend was gaining confidence now. 'And the food was even worse.'

'Listen to it – just *listen* to it!' The old crone was getting beside herself with rage.

'In fact, I think you should be reported to Equity,' Richard continued self-importantly, though neither of us was at that time a member of the theatre's own trades union.

'Report me? *Report me*! Oh, if only My George Albert was here now!'

'I'm not surprised he isn't,' Richard said. 'Not if you fed him bread-and-butter pudding every day of his life!'

I used that line to some effect a dozen years later when I wrote a little comedy called *Beside the Seaside*, and it always got one of the biggest laughs in the show.

After Ilfracombe came the Alhambra, Glasgow and the last week of my engagement, for I was to return to Leeds early in October. All the company and stage-management had become my fast friends, and I hated the thought of parting from them. I collected signed photographs from as many as I could, meaning to frame these myself and hang them up in my room at Devonshire Hall when I got back there. Our character-actress, Iris Fraser-Foss (and she was a good one), gave me a large, autographed picture of herself in *Smilin' Through* costume and wrote on the reverse of it: 'Hurry up and get your B.A. you B.F., and hurry back to us all. The Stage needs you. Love and good luck – Fossie, N.B.G.' No nicer thing has ever been said to me.

I stood in the wings on the Saturday night, after my final exit as Willie Ainley, to wait for the curtain-call. I looked round me at the stacked 'flats' against the rear wall, the braces and weights which are a concealed but indispensable part of any set-up, the props table to which I had just returned my personal properties and the arch that led off to the dressing-rooms with the sign *EXIT* above it, lit from within by a flicker of gas. I smelt again the smell of Theatre, a compound of scene-paint, size, make-up and sweat that every actor is familiar with, and I realised I loved the Stage with all my heart. Without thinking, I gritted my teeth and said out loud, 'I'll be back.'

'Shush!' came smartly from the prompt-corner; for the play was still going on, only a very few feet away. I shushed immediately.

My rainbow had dissolved, as all rainbows must, and I was filled with a sense of irretrievable loss. What I should have borne in mind then, and what I never forget today, is that rainbows simply come and go at will. You cannot catch a rainbow, and you can certainly never possess one. The most you can do is to be grateful for its beauty, its radiant promise and its inspiring company, and to hope, as it vanishes into the thinnest of thin air, that someday it may come your way again.

'Hold fast with open arms' is one of the finest pieces of advice I have ever heard. And it was not given to me by Grandma Sands. It came instead from a lady who has no part in this story, because she did not enter this part of my life. I was not to meet her for long years yet. But when she came, and come at last she did, her presence would transform my life and make it whole.

I had a week at home to gather my senses before starting my third and most important year at university, when the coveted degree of Bachelor of Arts (Hons. Eng.) might normally have come my way. Dad had long since completed his government training course and was now a fully fledged engineer, working on the manufacture of aircraft parts. Mother had gone back into the mill. And brother Bill, at thirteen, was nearing the end of his schooling at Lapage Street Modern. Bradford Moor had been swept clean of young men of my age, and I was glad when my brief visit was over and I could return to my old room at Devonshire Hall.

Within seven days, my call-up papers had arrived.

It was still early in the month, and I was ordered to report for duty on Tuesday 14 October. I put in the usual plea for deferment until I had taken my degree, and the Head of the English Department, Professor Wilfred Roland Childe, seemed quite hopeful of my prospects. 'It's not usual, of course, with arts students. On the other hand, you have quite a record. They *may* consider you a special case.' I saw no reason why they should, but nonetheless attended all my lectures, wrote the required essays and did all I could to exploit fully the few days of freedom I felt were left to me. On Friday 10 October I saw my professor again, to ask if he had any news. 'They've promised to give a definite decision on Monday,' he informed me. That would be the day before I was required to enlist, and I felt bound to comment: 'They're leaving it a bit late, sir.'

'They're leaving everything a bit late in this war, Mr Sands.' I had forgotten that he had seen distinguished service in the First World War, and was thus in a strong position to assess the conduct of the Second.

It goes without saying that I had to make all the necessary preparations for my call-up, whether it came or not. In my own mind I was certain now that it would.

That Friday night I took Diana out to see a Rooney-Garland film called *Babes in Arms* at the Tatler, and poured my heart out to her on our stroll afterwards to her bus-station. She was very sympathetic, but pointed out with characteristic candour: 'You're not the only one.'

But you are, you know, at a time like that. Whether the rest of the world recognises it or not, you *are* the only one. Because there is only one *you*.

'Will you write to me – as often as you can?' I was hoping for many letters.

'I'll write.' Her voice sounded offhand. 'But only now and then.' For some reason she hadn't called me 'darling' all evening.

'What's up?' I asked her.

'Nothing,' she said.

'Yes, there is.'

She looked me full in the face. 'Well, since you're probably leaving Leeds and changing your life anyway, you might as well know I don't want us to go on any longer. It doesn't work. Fresh starts, all round.'

'Like that, is it?' The bottom started to drop out of yet another world.

'You see, I've such a lot to do,' Diana went on. 'I don't want to stay in rep for ever, I'm better than that. I want absolute freedom, to go to London and really *get* somewhere. It's what I'm meant for.'

'What if they call you up too, in the long run? It's in all the papers that –'

'Oh, they'll never get me, darling.' At last the theatrical term of endearment she habitually used had found its way back into our conversation. 'I'll beat them to it – join Ensa, something like that.' I found myself wondering rather bitterly whether 'Emlyn', 'Larry' or even the redoubtable 'Noel' might somehow intercede on her behalf. 'Do you want to kiss me goodbye?' That touch was typical of her.

'Not much point, is there?'

'I s'pose not.' She gave me that crooked smile, the last for some considerable time, and when she squeezed my hand the gesture was warm enough. Just. 'Good luck, Leslie – here's my bus.'

She was another one who never called me 'Les'. The theatrical 'darling' never had quite the same appeal.

I think I made my mind up about something that night as I trudged back up the hill to Devonshire Hall. In future I would never again worship Woman from afar. No. In time to come I would respect her – deeply – from as close as I could get. This resolution, cynical as it may seem, was quite a good thing for me and kept my head above water for some few years after that. And that was just as well, because some of the water I got into tended to be rather hot.

I took my personal belongings home the next day, and said my farewells to all but the immediate family over the weekend.

'You'll be all right,' Grandma Sands told me, 'I think that university's put you right side up.'

At Seaton Street I found that Grandad Riley had recently suffered a nasty shock which he regarded as a personal affront from Adolf Hitler.

Bradford had few air-raids of its own during the course of the war, but German bombers often passed high overhead on their way to and from more vital targets; and air-raid warnings were annoyingly frequent, especially at night. Sirens in the daytime never seemed quite so death-dealing; and people tended to carry on with their normal pursuits when they sounded, instead of hurrying down to cellars for shelter and protection. One day my mother was cleaning the house after the warning had gone and Grandad Riley, to show his contempt for all things foreign, had gone clomping off across the little yard to the outside lavatory. Suddenly a single bomb was dropped by some marauder in the sky. It went off in the city centre with a bang that could be heard for miles around. Mother crouched under the table on hands and knees, frightened out of her wits as she afterwards freely admitted. Fortunately no further explosions were forthcoming, and shortly afterwards the all-clear went. She put the kettle on and waited for her father to return to the house now that the coast was clear. Minutes passed, and there was no sign of the old man. She opened the door and called across the square of garden: 'Dad! Cup o' tea. Come on, they've gone.' Silence reigned. Growing anxious, she crossed and tapped on the whitewashed wooden door. 'Dad! Dad, are you all right?' A deep and prolonged groan came from within, scaring her much more than the recent bomb had done. 'Dad, whatever's the matter?'

A long sigh came now, husky from the pipe-smoking, and deeply despairing. 'They've got me, lass. They've got me. I allus knew they would.'

'Don't be daft!' Mum was really upset now. 'That bomb fell down in t'town. Just undo this sneck and come out o' there.'

'I'll nivver stand up straight again.'

Fearing he might have suffered some kind of stroke, my poor mother found herself hammering on the lavatory door. 'Act right in your head. Come out o' there straightaway!'

Slowly ... very slowly ... the latch was lifted. The door opened ... and out staggered her father, almost in tears. He was indeed bent double.

'Nay, Dad. What's up wi' you?'

'I've told thee. It's their fault, the buggers! *I'll nivver stand up straight again.*'

'No, you won't.' My mother was shaking with laughter now. 'And do you know why? Just look – you've fastened one of your braces to your flies!'

He stared down at his trousers, and she was right. Unholy panic had made him use the wrong buttons – and that's why he couldn't stand up straight, like a man.

He never lived it down.

I locked all Diana's letters in a little tin trunk in the bedroom, along with my precious signed pictures from the tour. I wrapped my typewriter up in sacking and put it in the old clothes-cupboard that had once stabled my wooden rocking-horse called Tony, after Tom Mix's famous white stallion. I pressed my flannels, brushed my sports-jacket well and sponged down my aged raincoat. I checked my finances, and found there was almost fifteen pounds left from the money I had saved up during *Smilin' Through*. (I had been determined not to go into the Services with nothing to fall back on.) I gave some of this to my Mum and promised I would make her an allowance out of my pay, once I had settled in. I told brother Bill he could have the bike that Dad had bought me when I was eleven. And on Monday I went back to Leeds, to hear the verdict.

It was four o'clock in the afternoon before Professor Childe could see me.

'I'm sorry, Mr Sands. We did all we could but – well, you know how it is with arts students. They saw no reason why an exception should be made in your case.'

'Thank you for trying, sir.'

We shook hands, and he said: 'Come back to us when it's all over. Meanwhile – have a good war. I quite enjoyed mine, actually.' He still had to walk with a stick.

At five-to four I had been a university student and an ex-professional actor. At five-past I was a private citizen again, alone with the knowledge, down in black and white on my call-up papers, that if I did not report to the Reception Centre at Padgate by noon on the following day, I would be posted as a deserter. Apparently, they did not mince words in the Royal Air Force.

That was to be my last night at Seaton Street for some considerable time. Albert travelled over from Daisy Hill to say ta-ra and wish me well. I knew he would. 'You've shown 'em you can handle a pen, Les,' he said. 'Now show 'em you can handle a rifle.' I did not care to remind him that I was going to be trained as a radar-wireless mechanic (and God help all those radio sets to come). I hoped therefore that I would never be called upon to use firearms. I could still see that dead German my father had left in the dug-out long ago, with his kicked-in face.

My mother cried softly; she had no need to speak. My father's hand rested on my shoulder for a moment, but all he said was: 'Do your best, lad. Pity about that degree.' He paused for a second and then grinned. 'Hey – I was only thinking, tonight ... I'd love to go back in time to Barkerend School and tell 'em ... but never mind.' He went straight upstairs to bed, and he was stone-cold sober.

I caught a train the next morning to Warrington in Cheshire, and a bus from there to Padgate. Here for a time I ceased to be Leslie Sands, and became instead No. 1517684 in the R.A.F. It would be five years before I stepped on a professional stage again.

Chapter Fourteen

❖

Waiting in the Wings

'AIRMAN!'

I stopped dead in my tracks. The summons rang with authority, so I stood smartly to attention. This was not a complete success, since I was carrying in one hand my regulation pint pot, and in the other my 'irons' – the knife, fork and spoon I had been issued with on the day I joined. I must therefore have cut a rather comical figure on the middle concourse of the R.A.F. Station, Cranwell. The roar had arrested me when I was on my way back from the cookhouse to my billet in C Block, following a twenty-four hour guard duty in the wilds of fogbound Lincolnshire. During that time, I had assiduously kept watch (two hours on and four hours off) over an obsolescent Blenheim bomber with only a wooden rifle and a packet of Players to keep me company. I was very tired.

'AIRMAN!' The bellow was repeated. 'OVER HERE!'

I looked 'over there', and found myself gazing at the soapy visage of a warrant-officer, interrupted during his morning shave with a cut-throat razor, as he glared back at me furiously from the open window of his bunk. Next to the livid features streaked with blood and lather, and perched on a shelf that was exactly level with his head, was a white chamber-pot of giant dimensions.

'Yes?' I enquired, innocently.

'Yes – *what?*' The tone of voice, diminished in volume, was none the less ominous.

'Yes, *sir*?'

'What you doing there?'

'Just on my way to bed; I've been on guard duty,' I explained. 'Sir.' I added, just to be on the safe side.

'And what is that you're standing on, then?'

I looked down at my large black boots, baffled. I must have been very tired. 'The ground – ?' I ventured, mildly.

His broad face assumed the expression of a tortured martyr. 'That green stuff there – under your flat feet. That's GRASS, that is. GRASS!'

'Ah! Yes, sir.'

As if pained beyond endurance, he now asked me, 'Don't you never read D.R.O.'s, lad?'

I had a passing acquaintance with Daily Routine Orders, but had never made them my life's work. 'Er – yes.'

'You don't sound too sure. *Can* you read?'

I couldn't resist it. 'A bit.'

'D.R.O.'s emphasise – 'he relished the word, and decided to use it again to impress me, 'they *emphasise* that airmen shall keep off the grass AT ALL TIMES.'

'Sorry.' I jumped back, still at attention, on to the gravel path. I could no longer look him in the eyes and keep a straight face, so I shifted my gaze slightly away from his.

'What you staring at now?' He glanced to one side. 'Ah. You are concentrating – *concentrating* I say, on this!' He tapped the utensil beside him and it rang like an obedient bell.

'That's right, sir.'

'Ain't you never seen a po before?'

'Er, now and again.' I didn't know where to look.

'When I am addressing you,' and he was breathing hard now, 'you will look at my face – my *face* – and not my chamber-pot!'

'Right, sir.'

'What are you sniggering at?'

'I can't tell the difference.' It was out before I could stop it.

We held each other's eyes for a split-second, while the earth stood still. Then he exploded.

'YOU'RE ON A FUCKING CHARGE!!!'

It wasn't the first. It wouldn't be the last. And the charge was always the same: 'Conduct prejudicial to the good order and discipline of the Royal Air Force.' That covered everything. Before long I came to acknowledge that however hard you try, you can't beat the machine; so I gave up trying. But I never let it steam-roller over me. Gradually I realised that if you thought long enough and hard enough – there was always a way round it.

I served my King and Country as faithfully as I could for slightly less than five years (from 14 October 1941 to 12 August 1946) and did no credit to either of them whatsoever. Officially I was classed as a radar-wireless mechanic, Grade One. Thanks to a good memory, I knew all the theory of wireless telegraphy and radio telephony backwards, but – and I could have told them this before we started – I never did come to grips with the practice of them. Wires and screwdrivers, soldering-irons, valves and induction coils, conduits and condensers were all a complete mystery to me from start to finish. So I found a quick and efficient way round the necessary and infuriating handiwork. If a tricky problem came my way, I would simply rip the whole set from its moorings and return it to Maintenance Unit as 'completely unserviceable'. This got me quite a reputation as a perfectionist, and I was steadily promoted to a position where my duties consisted mainly of documentation and the ordering of others to do all the dirty work. That's the Service way.

I was never posted out of this country; and during the time I served, I was mainly attached to units of Bomber Command, especially those concerned with the training of aircrew in signals operations. Therefore I had a most undistinguished war career, and one which is not in the least worth setting down on paper. V.E. Day came at last, and I was jolly grateful.

Mention of V.E. Day reminds me that I found myself at its close in the saloon bar of the Angel and Royal Hotel,

Grantham. The whole world seemed to be drunk that night, though its intoxication sprang mainly from relief. Along with some Service colleagues I had scaled the front of a civic building that afternoon, and we had captured from its summit a large and tattered Union Jack; I sat draped in this and a pink haze of alcohol as I surveyed the passing parade, in search of what was once called 'talent'.

The blonde in the far corner was quite dazzling in her bright green Land Army sweater, red neckerchief and skin-tight riding-breeches; and there was no doubt she had some interest in me, tipsy though I was. But our attempts at communication were furtive, and hampered by the presence of a sailor at her table who seemed to have a prior claim on her. This beefy individual finally felt the call of nature and, with much pushing and foul-mouthed shoving, went off outside to relieve himself. As if by magic, the Land Army girl appeared in front of me.

'What are you doing here?' she said cheekily.

'What's it look like?' I told her, 'I'm celebrating. Aren't we all?'

She shifted the Union Jack and slid on to my knee, folding one side of the giant flag round her shapely figure. 'Won the war all by yourself then, did you? Is this your decoration?'

'I had a bit of help from the Yanks. Not a lot, though.'

All of a sudden she flung her arms round me and gave me a great big smacking kiss. Then she drew back. 'You don't know me, do you?' She smiled, slyly. 'We've met before, you and me – we have, you know!'

I was ready to take her word for it, and anyway this would save a lot of spadework – so I kissed her back, and this time made a longer job of it. 'Fancy meeting you!' I said, and settled down to pick up where we might have left off.

Before we could make much real progress, her escort for the evening had reappeared. His lowering look roamed the crowded room. He saw us, and forced his way over. Swaying heavily, he leaned across the blonde and breathed beer into my face. 'What you on, boyo? She came in here with me.'

I took a deep breath. At close quarters he was more of a sea-mastiff than a sea-dog, and I didn't really fancy my chances.

I needn't have worried, for the Land Army had lost none of its customary presence of mind. 'It's all right, Arthur,' she consoled him. 'We know each other – it's me cousin!'

I nearly laughed out loud remembering, as I instantly did, Pat Harker's identical stratagem in a faraway milk bar some long years before. But the very able-bodied seaman wasn't even smiling. 'Pull the other one,' he rasped, and leaned in even closer. His breath was very stale.

'It's right!' the blonde insisted. 'It's our Les, all the way from Bradford.' She pinched both my cheeks and giggled. 'You didn't even know me, did you? I'm your Cousin May from Mosscar Street.'

I had last seen her when she was a tousle-headed moppet of ten. I never felt a bigger fool in all my life.

Now that peace had broken out, there came the immense and complicated task of demobilising millions of Servicemen; and this involved their necessary rehabilitation for the return to civilian life. Various programmes were instituted for this purpose by the Services, and the R.A.F.'s contribution was the setting up of its Educational and Vocational Training Scheme. This earned my gratitude, for it resulted in my leaving the detested world of technology and becoming a flight-sergeant instructor in English Language and Literature. Those were my best days in the 'Air Works', when I felt at last I was doing something worthwhile that had as its prime object the helping of my fellowmen and not their planned destruction.

I had been at Cranwell, the self-styled 'cradle of the R.A.F.', since mid-1943; and it was beginning to assume the status of a second home. Now that I felt I was using my time instead of merely slaving it away, I began to grow more fond of its College, its redbrick barrack-blocks, its Naafis and its sprawling training-schools. In my off-duty hours, together with a corporal called Peter Sallis (still a great friend, and now a very famous actor) and an attractive, talented actress called Maureen Shaw, I built up The Little Theatre. This was a thriving amateur concern which, during my last year or so in uniform, presented a dozen or more shows in the Station Cinema. We were always blessed with packed houses, and in due course toured other Air Force bases, Naval establishments and Army camps with selected attractions from our repertoire. This extended from Shakespeare via *Pygmalion* to such unashamedly commercial offerings as *Murder Without Crime* and *French Without Tears*. The Little Theatre's career began with J.B. Priestley's *I Have Been Here Before* and ended shortly before my demobilisation with the same play, a piece that has regularly punctuated my theatrical life. Further, on this Station I struck up a friendship with the Gas Officer, in civilian life a professional actor called Walter Wade, and together we collaborated in the writing of a farcical comedy with the title of *Men Of Good Name*. This was honoured with its first – and last – presentation at the Little Theatre. It gave the two of us a lot of laughs, and got me accustomed to using my typewriter again after four somewhat fallow years.

Spurred on by the comedy's reception I settled down, sometimes between lectures and rehearsals, and often in the wee small hours of the morning, to writing a play of my own. This was, in a phrase culled from the old days, 'a human story of laughter and tears', which dealt with the return to university of a student after long and demanding active service. Its sources will be obvious. And it will come as no surprise that I finally christened it *The Missing Years*.

Also at Cranwell – when I had absolutely no time to call my own and after many colourful affaires, most of them too casual to remember – true adult love made itself known to me for the first time in my life.

Although English by birth, Corporal Fresson hailed from Inverness, where her father had in peacetime been a senior pilot with a civilian airline; so it was only natural that she should have joined the Women's Auxiliary Air Force. She was with the Transport Section, and became the A.O.C.'s own choice as his personal driver. The Station Commander's batman kept chickens, and this meant that Betty had ready

I Have Been Here Before – the first Little Theatre production.

Poster from the author's collection

access to a good supply of free-range eggs. The Naafi was always ready to cook these for her, and I observed this enviable 'perk' one night in the canteen. Mainly to taste a decent egg or two for a change, I forced myself boldly on her attentions. Before long, the two of us were very much in love.

To me, she was always 'Bet'. Her figure was slight but perfectly proportioned, and she was very attractive. Her hair was brown and her eyes were hazel, flecked with green. She was the only one I ever met who could make a Waaf cap and greatcoat look trim, smart and ultra-feminine all at the same time. She had a warm personality, a lively intelligence and a delightful sense of humour. I can truly say I was the envy of many of my colleagues when Bet and I went about together. And I honestly believe she came to care for me deeply and sincerely.

She completely failed to understand my obsessive ambitions, at first. But then I told her all about my background, and how much my betterment meant to me. After that she sympathised entirely, and did all in her power to help me. Also, I think she realised how desperate I was to become my own man again, after those interminable years in uniform. We were inseparable for over eighteen months, and for most of that time we were lovers and good friends, a combination that sadly does not always happen.

But when demobilisation came along, Betty was twenty four. That, she felt, was an age when a woman should be married and raising her own family. It was a perfectly natural and laudable attitude, and she seemed sure at the time that I was the man she wanted, to share her life. But on this one issue of children we differed crucially. In my own selfish view I had lost five whole years of my working life, and had a lot of making-up to do before I could even consider taking on things as serious as family responsibilities. This of course was in the days before trial marriages and so-called 'commitments' existed. If you walked down the aisle with someone then, you were expected to keep the promises you made. The biggest vow I had undertaken up to this point had been to myself and my future – and I was determined that it must be kept, come hell or high water. So I mentally ran away from a union that, in my totally self-centred opinion, might well have turned into a shackle.

Betty's release came. She left Cranwell and went back into civilian life. Almost immediately, the rot set in. If one can stifle love, then that is what I did. Without conscience, I deliberately and ruthlessly set out to seek consolation for her absence, whenever and wherever it could be found. Word of my transgressions got through to her, sent by mutual friends on the Station, and that was the end of our relationship. I admired her for her blunt ultimatum ... and I let her go.

My love for Betty cut deep within me, and I cannot even now understand how I could have treated her with a callousness that was unforgivable. I have no excuse. All I can say is that that's the way I was, then. I know (through those same mutual friends) that she joined the Control Commission and went to Germany, where she met and married a Dane who gave her the family she so much wanted and deserved.

The pity of it is, Bet, you were never quite able to come to terms with the demon inside that everlastingly drove me on. That was no fault of yours ... I couldn't properly handle it myself at that time. All things being equal (and they very rarely are) you were well rid of me, and that's a solid fact.

The August of 1946 brought my own demobilisation. The degree of Bachelor of Arts had been conferred on me three years earlier ('awarded under the Emergency Statute whereby allowance may be made for approved national service'), and I was informed by the University of Leeds that I would be welcome back there for the year's study for a Diploma in Education. Following that, I could start full-time teaching at high-school level. At the same time, I knew that on the great day of release I should be entitled to four weeks of demob pay and a gratuity of some eighty-five pounds for my five years 'service' with the Forces.

My future, it seemed, hung in the balance. On the one hand, I could have a settled life teaching the subject I loved; on the other, I could take a blind stab at a precarious career in show business. But when I looked into my heart, there was no choice at all.

So I asked to be demobbed not in the North of England, but at R.A.F. Uxbridge; that was a damned sight nearer to Shaftesbury Avenue and I would save a lot on train fares.

I arrived in London on a bright August morning and booked in at the Coram Hotel, a bed-and-breakfast establishment in Bloomsbury. Next morning, the search for work began. I told myself to be practical. The hunt must only continue for as long as the money held out. After that – no Labour Exchanges, certainly – but a return to Leeds, and the comfortable scholastic life. I wonder if I could ever have kept to that?

For a few days I haunted theatreland, gazing at the glossy photographs outside West End theatres, studying the names up there in lights, and trying to storm the fastnesses of agents' offices. I found out where the actors congregated and visited their pubs and coffee-bars, drinking shandies and glasses of milk, my ears pricked to glean any information about forthcoming productions. I tried, most unsuccessfully, to develop a veneer of sophistication. I was yet to learn that although it is a world of make-believe, what really and ultimately works in the theatre is the truth and nothing but the truth. I remember a flashy thespian, so effeminate he could never have seen the inside of a cookhouse, making a pass at me at the S.F. Grill in Denman Street. He seemed quite sympathetic. 'So you're trying to get in, dear boy? Well, I don't envy you. You haven't done anything, and you don't know anyone. You see, what counts in The Theatre is good connections. Now if we really got to know one another ... I mean, *really* ... I might introduce you to one or two people who could be useful. I mean it! *Good connections*, that's all you need.'

I didn't need anything, not the way he was pointing. 'The only good connection I ever had,' I told him briefly, 'was the umbilical cord – and that was severed at birth.'

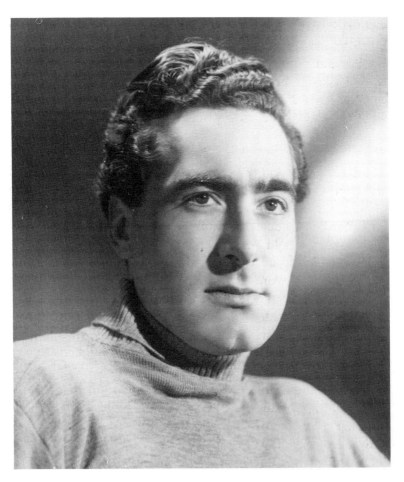

'So you want to be an actor, do you?' *Photo: Author's collection*

And then came a friendly call from Walter Wade, my erstwhile co-author at Cranwell: 'Tennent's are holding auditions for Shakespeare at the Piccadilly this week. I've spoken to Bill Conway about you. He's one of their managers, and he's put your name forward. Get over there tomorrow and try your luck.'

H.M. Tennent Ltd, under the leadership of the redoubtable 'Binkie' Beaumont, were the biggest producers of fashionable hits in the West End, and specialised in the lavish presentation of classical plays. I spent a busy evening closeted in my hotel-room, brushing up my Shakespeare with a vengeance.

At ten o'clock sharp the following morning I was at the Piccadilly Theatre. Down in the wings, I sought out the assistant stage-manager. She was a little scared rabbit with long, bronze-coloured hair, called Barbara.

'I'm sorry, Mr Sands – I can't find your name down here.'

'It's there somewhere,' I assured her. 'Mind you, it's all been fixed up in a hurry ... '

As she glanced back again at her clipboard, I looked about me. The off-stage areas were jammed with actors. They came in all shapes and sizes, all of them were striking in looks, and most of them seemed to be very well-dressed. I found myself wishing that my Service haircut weren't so obvious, and that my demob suit (Burton's, medium grey with a heavy chalk-stripe) had turned out to be a better fit. Still, all that couldn't be helped. Under powerful lights on the deep stage nearby an immaculate aspirant, who looked like a Greek god dressed by Savile Row, was declaiming Hamlet's soliloquy in beautifully modulated tones.

'You're not on the list. Definitely. Not for today.' Barbara's voice was as adamant as a frightened but conscientious rabbit's could be. 'And if your name's not down here, you can't go on.'

'Look, Babs – ' I tried to sound both gentle and firm; I was acting my head off, and it was beginning to work. 'My agents fixed this,' I lied, glibly. 'What's more, I have another appointment. Can't hang about here all morning.'

'I'm so sorry.' Her eyes grew large with concern, and I knew I was winning.

'When they start screaming for me, tell them I was here, will you? And tell 'em why I left.' I turned for the swing-doors.

'Mr Sands ... ' Young Barbara had a note of pleading now. 'I'm really sorry – but it's not my fault.'

'Barbara, love.' I took her by the shoulders. 'When they hear about this, heads will roll. All I can say is, I'll tell them you only did your duty, *as you saw it*.' And I carried on out.

'Mr Sands – Leslie!' I stopped, with my back to her. There was a second of suspense and then she hissed: 'I'm putting you on next.'

Knocking at the knees, I gave them 'Friends, Romans, countrymen ... ' and after it there was a short, whispered discussion in the stalls. The gathering out front, I later learned, included Daphne Rye the casting director, Elsie Beyer the general manager and the very distinguished director, Glen Byam Shaw. The play they were auditioning for was *Antony and Cleopatra* and would star the matinée idols Godfrey Tearle and Edith Evans.

I stood in the middle of the stage, on tenterhooks.

'Have you anything else?' the casting-chief asked me.

'I once played Coriolanus.'

'Carry on, then,' she invited. And I was halfway through the second extract before she broke me off, with: 'That's fine. Let's see your legs.'

'I beg your pardon?' I gawped into the auditorium, but because of the stage-lighting all I could make out were dim shapes that had no faces.

'Your legs! Not ashamed of them, are you?'

Wondering what the hell was going on, I carefully removed the double-breasted jacket of my new suit, laid it on a nearby chair, and pulled my braces down off my shoulders. I was about to undo my flies when a shout of laughter came from the front.

'There's no need to strip off, Mr – er – '

'Sands,' Embarrassment made my voice curt. 'My name is Leslie Sands.'

'This isn't the Windmill. Just roll the trouser legs half-way up.'

They were looking for people who could play small parts and whose legs were thick enough not to look ridiculous under the brevity of a Roman kilt.

It transpired that Bill Conway had done his stuff and my name was duly down – but for the following day. I would have been informed of this by telephone, had I not taken Walter Wade's tip, jumped the gun in my eagerness, and turned up at the Piccadilly on the very first day of auditions. I gathered all this when Walter rang the Coram Hotel the following evening.

'Never mind, the great news is – you're in! Don't worry, you'll be hearing from them.'

251

When the momentous letter arrived, I took it up to Yorkshire with me to show the family; I was on a flying visit to see how they all were, and to pick up what few spare clothes I possessed.

'So it's acting, after all?' my father said.

'It's got to be, Dad,' I told him. 'I s'pose I'm off me rocker, but –'

'You know your own know best.' He half-smiled, and I knew he was still on my side and always would be. 'Think on, though – don't expect miracles.' He sounded exactly like his mother.

I was sorry I could not talk it over with Grandma Sands, but she had left us during the very last year of hostilities. My commanding officer couldn't release me for the day of her funeral, but had given me an immediate twenty-four hours' 'compassionate'. I had hitch-hiked up to Bradford to pay my last respects.

When I had arrived at 196 Barkerend Road one of my uncles had been in attendance downstairs, in the large and gloomy living-room I knew so well.

… Uncle Lennie (Grandma's second son) wore carpet slippers for the occasion, and was smoking his customary Woodbine.

'D'you mind going up by yourself, Les? I've been trailing up and down them steps all day long.'

'No, I don't mind at all.'

'She allus liked you, you know. Funny, that. She didn't take to many people – didn't trust a soul!' He sank back on the horsehair sofa and took another thoughtful drag at his cigarette. 'Not even family,' he added, with a sourness that spoke volumes.

I didn't answer him, but went out through the open chamber-door and up the wide stone staircase.

She lay in the vast double bed, as still and unapproachable as stone. Sunlight filtered unwillingly through two dusty windows. There was a glass on the bedside table with her false teeth in it; and next to that, a jug of water that would never now be drunk. She seemed shrunken in death, but the old grim look was still there; and her bloodless lips seemed tightly compressed as if, even at the moment of extinction, she had been criticising the Lord for the time he had chosen to take her soul. 'They only come here when they want summat,' echoed in my mind from a far distance. This time, all I had come for was to say goodbye. I bent my head over hers, and kissed the ice-cold forehead I would never see again …

And so I had left her, with only a vase of fresh daffodils for company. They were a present from my mother, who had faithfully kept her promise to lay the old lady out.

Goodnight and God Bless, Grandma. And thank you.

It was nearing midnight and the family had all gone to bed, when I refilled my old fountain-pen and sat down to re-read the Tennent offer before putting my name to it. I had been determined that this moment should be savoured alone, and to the full. H.M. Tennent Ltd invited me to play Silius, who had one appearance only and a sum total of eleven lines of blank verse; I would be expected to understudy Enobarbus and the Cleopatra Messenger, and rehearsals would commence in three weeks' time; my salary would be fifteen pounds a week.

This was the first written contract I had ever had, and my heart was beating faster than usual as I signed it. We had no blotting-paper. As I waited for the ink to dry, I sat back in my chair and looked into the dying fire. My thoughts went back in time to the wings of a draughty old theatre in Glasgow, and to the pledge I had made there five long years before.

That promise had finally been kept. And now – for better or for worse – I was back where I belonged.

THEATRE ROYAL

GLASGOW   'Phone: Douglas 6822

Proprietors: Howard & Wyndham Ltd.

Chairman & Man. Dir.: A. Stewart Cruikshank   Man.: J. G. Stewart

ONE WEEK COMMENCING MONDAY, OCTOBER 28th
NIGHTLY at 7 o'clock   MATINEES: WED. & SAT. at 2 o'clock

Prices of Admission (including Tax): Boxes, 36/-, 32/-, 18/-; Stalls 9/-, 6/6;
Grand Circle 8/-, 6/6; Pit Stalls 4/-; Upper Circle 4/6, 3/6;
Balcony 2/-, 1/6

TENNENT PLAYS LTD.

In association with THE ARTS COUNCIL OF GREAT BRITAIN

PRESENTS

EDITH   GODFREY
EVANS   TEARLE

IN

WILLIAM SHAKESPEARE'S

ANTONY AND
CLEOPATRA

GEORGE HOWE   GIBB McLAUGHLIN

DAVID GREENE   JOHN FRANKLYN   LESLIE SANDS   GEORGE CARR
JAMES CAIRNCROSS   ROYDEN GODFREY   PAUL HARDWICK   JAMES WELLMAN

MARK DIGNAM   MICHAEL GOODLIFFE

HUGH METCALFE   PATRICK ROSS   JAMES BAILEY   RICHARD SCOTT
NANCY NEVINSON   DAVID SPENSER   PETER WILLIAMS   DOUGLAS WILMER

HELEN CHRISTIE   OLAF POOLEY

RICHARD WARNER   GORDON LITTMAN   MICHAEL KENT   KATHERINE BLAKE
ARNOLD DIAMOND   JOHN CADELL   PHILIP GUARD

ANTHONY QUAYLE

Directed by GLEN BYAM SHAW
Decor by MOTLEY

PRIOR TO OPENING AT THE
PICCADILLY THEATRE, LONDON
ON WEDNESDAY DECEMBER 18th